Trends in Advanced Avionics

Trends in Advanced Avionics

JIM CURRAN

 Iowa State University Press / Ames

Jim Curran specializes in functional analysis and research on evolving avionics capability. A systems engineer with a major avionics company, he is a senior member of the Institute of Electrical and Electronics Engineers and of the Society of Logistics Engineers. Curran, a longtime pilot, is a gold-seal flight instructor and also holds an airline transport pilot license.

Authorization to photocopy items for internal or personal use, or the internal or personal use of specific clients, is granted by Iowa State University Press, provided that the base fee of $.10 per copy is paid directly to the Copyright Clearance Center, 27 Congress Street, Salem, MA 01970. For those organizations that have been granted a photocopy license by CCC, a separate system of payment has been arranged. The fee code for users of the Transactional Reporting Service is 0-8138-0749-2/92 $.10.

∞ Printed on acid-free paper in the United States of America

First edition, 1992

Library of Congress Cataloging-in-Publication Data
Curran, Jim
    Trends in advanced avionics / Jim Curran. – 1st ed.
        p. cm.
    Includes bibliographical references and index.
    ISBN 0-8138-0749-2
    1. Avionics. I. Title.
TL695.C87   1992
629.135 – dc20   92-5963

Photo on pages 2 and 3, Global Express cockpit, courtesy of Canadair.

To Mary,

whose support has been long and strong,

and to Jamison and Christopher,

for sharing computer time

CONTENTS

Foreword, *James Rankin*, viii

Preface, x

1. **Introduction, 5**
   1.1. Purpose of Avionics, 5
   1.2. Nature of Avionics, 6
   1.3. Major Trends, 8
   1.4. Preview, 9

2. **Framework of Avionics Development, 12**
   2.1. User Acceptance, 12
   2.2. Air Traffic Control Environment, 14
   2.3. Technology Factors, 19
   2.4. Political and Regulatory Aspects, 36
   2.5. Business Concerns, 45
   2.6. Summary, 48

3. **Review of Advanced Avionics Programs, 51**
   3.1. Avionics Programs: Pave Pillar, Pave Sprinter, Pave Pace, ICNIA, Pilot's Associate, Supercockpit, 51
   3.2. Aircraft Programs: ATF, ATA, ATB, RAH, EFA, 777, NASP/HSCT, FSX, 59
   3.3. Spillover from Advanced Avionics Programs, 73
   3.4. Summary, 73

4. **System-level Advances, 75**
   4.1. System Integration, 75
   4.2. Automation, 84
   4.3. Summary, 89

5. **Crew-System Interfaces, 91**
   5.1. General, 91
   5.2. Multipurpose Units, 92
   5.3. Displays, 94
   5.4. Speech Recognition and Synthesis, 101
   5.5. Directional Sound, 102
   5.6. Switching, 102
   5.7. Operational Simplicity, 104
   5.8. Summary, 110

6. Navigation Advances, 112
  6.1. Historical View, 112
  6.2. Satellite-based Navigation (Satnav), 114
  6.3. Inertial Navigation, 118
  6.4. Terrain-referenced Navigation, 119
  6.5. Terminal-area Navigation, 120
  6.6. Airmass Navigation, 124
  6.7. Radar, 126
  6.8. Summary, 127

7. Communication Advances, 129
  7.1. Introduction, 129
  7.2. Air-Ground Coordination, 130
  7.3. Transponder Datalink Communication, 132
  7.4. Satellite Communication (Satcom), 134
  7.5. Aeronautical Telecommunication Network, 138
  7.6. Collision-alerting Communication, 139
  7.7. Summary, 143

8. Flight Control Advances, 144
  8.1. Introduction, 144
  8.2. Fly-by-Wire, 145
  8.3. Fly-by-Light (Fiber Optics), 147
  8.4. Sidestick Controller, 148
  8.5. Autoland Capability, 149
  8.6. Windshear Avoidance and Recovery, 151
  8.7. Other Flight Control Advances, 153
  8.8. Summary, 154

9. Perspectives on the Future, 156
  9.1. Introduction, 156
  9.2. Avionics Trends, 156
  9.3. Evolutionary Trends, 162
  9.4. Information Age, 164
  9.5. Integration, 166
  9.6. Automation, 170
  9.7. Postscript, 172

Acronyms and Abbreviations, 175
References, 183
Index, 187

FOREWORD

The technology base in avionics has shifted from analog to digital circuitry, displays have evolved from electromechanical to CRT to flat panels, system architectures are shifting from the conventional LRU-based independent approach to a more integrated, modular, and centralized approach, and functionality is now implemented largely in software rather than hardware. The first glass-cockpit, digital commercial aircraft were the Boeing 757 and 767. Major avionics systems that evolved out of those 1970 advances, such as the flight control system, flight management system, and the electronic flight instrument system, contributed to the advent of the two-crew cockpit.

In the 1980s airframe manufacturers and avionics designers concentrated on improving the new generation of digital avionics. Increased integration and automation led to new results and problems. More functional capability became available. Powerful processors and dense solid-state memory devices allowed designers to achieve more impressive functions and system performance, sometimes at the cost of increasing crew workload and the risk of distraction. The 1980s also saw the development of earth-orbit satellites bringing continuous, reliable, worldwide navigation and communication to aviation, regardless of weather conditions, time of day, or remoteness of region. The traffic-alert and collision-avoidance system (TCAS), also developed in the 1980s, has improved in-flight safety in increasingly dense skies. Device-level technology heralded an era of highly integrated modular avionics systems.

This brings us to the present and the future. Today massive amounts of information from multichannel datalinks and onboard electronic library capability are being harnessed to support the crew's need to access complete information quickly. The Age of Information, however, has created an overload for pilots during the busiest phases of flight. Avionics designers are now addressing this problem with judicious applications of *human-centered automation* and system approaches that support *workload management* and *situation awareness*—three common buzzwords of today's avionics.

As Jim Curran explains, the 1990s will lead to cockpits with large, panoramic, solid-state displays that provide intuitive, graphical, informational displays. Avionics systems will begin to be integrated with the human element of *cockpit resource management*—another buzzword of modern aviation. Terminal navigation capability with enhanced vision sensors will improve arrival rates and safety. Windshear-detection sensors and fly-by-wire flight control systems will further improve safety and operational efficiency. Next-generation, integrated avionics systems will be characterized by fault-tolerant functional availability achieved through reconfigurable redundancy.

Curran's background in commercial and military avionics systems design enables him to cover advanced avionics in both arenas. He deals with developments in navigation, communication, and flight control systems, as well as with advances in air traffic control that will affect onboard systems. The book will be a necessary tool for avionics systems engineers in the 1990s and beyond.

James M. Rankin
Associate Professor of Electrical Engineering
St. Cloud State University, Minn.

PREFACE

As a longtime pilot and flight instructor, I am a user — and a critic — of avionics. As an avionics systems engineer with a specialty in functional analysis and definition, I am a contributor to the avionics specification and design process. Both my personal and professional interests are tied to developing avionics that can best serve the aviation industry.

In this review of advances in functional capability and performance, my primary interest is to describe the trends in avionics systems and the issues associated with them. Until the 1990s the trends in avionics functionality have been divergent. In the 1990s, however, the major trend is converging and consolidating avionics functions in highly integrated systems. This is a significant shift for the avionics field and the primary focus of this book.

My discussion focuses on major trends in the areas of communication, navigation, flight control, and integrated avionics management systems. It also examines advances in the underlying technology that make these trends possible and considers current programs to describe the kinds of avionics being planned now for tomorrow's aircraft.

Two colleagues, Lynn Cole and Dale March, reviewed the manuscript, and I thank them for their helpful comments. James Skiles, professor emeritus of electrical engineering at the University of Wisconsin-Madison, and an experienced, avid pilot, critiqued the manuscript in detail (even while on vacation in Hawaii) and encouraged its publication. Captain W. Van Wormer gave me the benefit of his hours in the cockpit contemplating avionics functionality from the pilot's perspective. Captain Steve Last also provided valuable suggestions based on his involvement in avionics functional definition throughout its significant evolutionary period. I am indebted to these and to hundreds of other pilots, avionics engineers, and aerospace colleagues from whose work I have benefited. I am grateful, too, to Jane Zaring, Bill Silag, and others at ISU Press for their support throughout the publication process. Finally, I would like to thank Mary Russell Curran for applying her professional editorial experience to these pages.

Trends in Advanced Avionics

DALE DUNN 10/91

1. Introduction

1.1. Purpose of Avionics

The trend toward increasing air travel continues. In 1990 the air transport system in the United States carried about 1.3 million passengers a day, with expectations of 2.5 million a day (nearly 1 billion passengers a year) by the year 2000. Likewise, the number of worldwide air passengers is projected to double by the year 2000, reaching 2 billion per year, and to double again by the year 2015. What makes this growth possible is a large, growing fleet of comfortable and safe aircraft and an extensive, sophisticated, worldwide air traffic control network. The aircraft fleet is well equipped and is becoming even better equipped with aviation electronics—avionics—that support the basic goal of helping flight crews get safely from point of departure to destination.

Pilots have a saying that covers their responsibilities in the cockpit, "aviate, navigate, communicate"—in that order. *Aviate* has to do with tracking and controlling the aircraft's pitch, roll, yaw, heading, airspeed, and altitude. *Navigate* has to do with several functions: tracking the aircraft's present position, position change (progress), ground track, and deviation from desired course; determining wind, drift correction, and waypoint estimates; tracking and avoiding—or else navigating safely through or around—frontal movements, precipitation, turbulence, windshear, microburst hazards, and other problematic weather; and finally, avoiding collision with obstacles, the terrain itself, and other aircraft. *Communicate* has to do with coordinating flight situation and progress with others who need to know, such as other crewmembers, ATC (air traffic control), other aircraft, FSS (flight service stations), and company dispatch control. It is the function of avionics systems to receive and display nav data, sense flight parameters, correlate information, consolidate and present information to the crewmembers, support crewmembers by automating functions such as flight control and flight management, enhance safety, improve flight performance, and permit communication with external elements. The purpose of individual avionics units can be associated with the cockpit functions of aviating, navigating, and communicating. A new category of avionics capability is emerging to help crews manage workload, onboard systems, and the flight situation.

The ultimate goal of avionics is to help an aircraft get from one location to another in almost any weather conditions. Inasmuch as humans still retain the final responsibility for operating an aircraft, avionics systems ease the pilot's task by facilitating communication between the pilot and external elements. Throughout this book I assume a human pilot will still be needed in the cockpit of the future. Certainly in terms of pure technical feasibility the avionics can efficiently and safely control an aircraft while taking off, flying enroute, and landing; in some cases the precision of autopilots exceeds the control capability of pilots. However, since this book is intended to be a realistic anticipation of future avionics, I will take into account realistic constraints, such as passenger demand that a human pilot be in control of the aircraft. When an aircraft travels hundreds of miles per hour through the atmosphere, which itself behaves in a somewhat nondeterministic way, when collision avoidance depends at least partly on the human "see-and-avoid" principle, and when legal liabilities are an ever-present concern, it is hard to imagine that there will ever be a day when the human pilot is removed from all roles in the cockpit.

1.2. Nature of Avionics

The field of avionics has been undergoing a metamorphosis on several fronts. Some changes are accelerating, and this process promises to continue. I intend to describe the areas in which these changes are occurring and provide an explanation of why they are happening. In such a dynamic field as avionics, which depends so heavily on the even more dynamic field of electronic technology, it is tempting to extrapolate the advances that are taking place now into the foreseeable future and beyond. I will indulge in this temptation; however, where I venture into the unforeseeable future it will be cautiously, knowing that others who have done so have often failed to account correctly for real-world constraints. In avionics, like many fields, these constraints include business and political realities.

Any exploration of avionics today must also review applicable advanced avionics military projects and note how relevant advances will be applied to commercial avionics. In discussing the future, though, one must temper futuristic concepts with what flight crews really need and what buyers can justify.

When the Wright brothers were developing the first controllable powered airplane in the first decade of the twentieth century, they used no avionics. At that time there were no electronics of any kind, much less aviation electronics. Cockpit instrumentation, of which avionics is a special category, was born out of need. For example, probably the first "instrument" was a piece of cotton twine hung with a weight on a 1909 Wright airplane to indicate yawing slips and skids as well as to provide a sense of airspeed. It helped the pilot perform a task related to flying the airplane with aerodynamic efficiency. Naturally, pilots desired more and more information about aircraft attitude, engine condition, and navigational situations. Pilots needed to know where they were fairly precisely, what their heading and ground track were, what their groundspeed was, and how far they might be deviating from their desired course. Avionics filled this need for information.

In the early days of aviation, airplane engines were notoriously undependable, and off-airport landings were common occurrences. Improvements in engine reliability and airframes (structures, coverings, and control mechanisms) dominated airplane research and design into the 1950s, until the advent of modern jet aircraft. As avionics came of age in the 1960s, and especially as digital technology was applied to avionics, the broad field of avionics began to play a role equal to that of airframes and engines. The need for sophisticated avionics capability in the military world did much to foster advanced avionics capability for commercial and general aviation applications also. It seems likely that "the potential for quantum improvements in avionics compared to other system constituents means that avionics will henceforth be as important as, if not more important than, airframe and engines in establishing the mission performance, reliability, and supportability" (Borky 1987, 10). In the early 1990s we are already finding that avionics systems can be up to 50 percent of the cost of an advanced military aircraft program.

Perhaps the avionics story really begins with the first electromechanical aircraft instruments. Although com and nav radios existed prior to these complex instruments, it was the unique aviation functionality of these instruments that led to sophisticated avionics. Philanthropist Daniel Guggenheim and his son, Harry, in addition to promoting and publicizing aviation in the 1920s, specifically funded research in the area of "fog flying," or flying by reference to instruments only. In July 1928 their fund requested that the army assign test pilot Jimmy Doolittle to this program. Instrument makers Elmer Sperry, Jr., and Paul Kollsman were hired to develop the artificial horizon, gyrocompass, and precision altimeter—three instruments to provide the kind of information that still dominates instrument flying today. The project was successful, and on September 24, 1929, Doolittle completed a test flight on Long Island that included takeoff and landing by reference to instruments with a radio navigational aid (Leary 1989, 31). Modern electronic versions of early electromechanical and pneumatic instruments are what first pushed sophisticated avionics to the forefront in today's state-of-the-art aircraft. The trends in modern avionics have their roots in early aircraft instrumentation. My goal is to describe what has evolved from these roots and to project readers' thoughts to tomorrow's avionics capability.

1.3. Major Trends

Certain technical trends in avionics are already clear. They include:

- Movement from analog to universal digital processing
- Increased levels of system monitoring, fault detection, and fault isolation
- Reduced equipment size, weight, and power consumption
- Increased reliability and maintainability
- More modularization of system hardware and software for better growth enhancement, survivability, and functional availability
- Higher levels of commonality and standardization of hardware for logistics purposes
- Increased device integration and miniaturization
- Movement from electromechanical to electronic flight instrument system (EFIS) displays
- More integration at the subsystem and functional levels, such as sensor fusion and integrated image processing
- Higher-tech approaches to functions, such as datalink instead of voice com, fly-by-wire instead of mechanical/hydraulic flight control systems, satcom and satnav instead of their ground-based counterparts, flat-panel displays instead of electromechanical and cathode ray tube (CRT) displays
- Increased information correlation, validation, sharing, and distribution
- Expanded functional capability and operational integration
- Increased flight safety support
- Pilot workload management through higher levels of functional, human-centered automation
- More information availability in a more intuitive graphical presentation (format/symbology)

Many of these trends-in-the-making are not yet fully realized. As they continue to develop, they will restructure the field of avionics and will serve as catalysts for new and more powerful trends. I hope to identify those current trends that by virtue of their mainstay value will be long-lived and will lead toward long-range trends in advanced avionics.

Long-range trends are never completely clear; articulating them becomes an informed crystal-ball exercise. In this age of rapid technological advancement, the trick is not to restrain the imagination when predicting the future but to free it. The foreseeable future is too close. We need to see beyond it to move in the right directions and to achieve the capability that is possible.

1.4. Preview

Navigation, communication, and flight control are the core functions of avionics. System-level advances and crew-system interfaces overlap and encompass all three functions. Figure 1.1 suggests the complexity of this interaction and indicates that avionics programs also develop within a large, comprehensive framework.

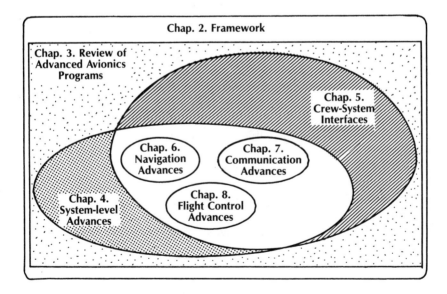

Figure 1.1. Topical relationships

Chapter 2 looks at elements in the framework — various technological factors, political and regulatory influences, and the business climate. Difficult as it is to predict the future, it is even more difficult to make forecasts when the trends depend on factors that are themselves somewhat volatile and uncertain, such as government stimulation of technology.

Much is already being planned and accomplished in several advanced aircraft and avionics programs, mostly spearheaded by the government. These programs will do a good deal to establish advanced avionics concepts and to lay the technological groundwork necessary for other avionics advances. Chapter 3, "Review of Advanced Avionics Programs," examines many of these programs and the impact each could have on the future of avionics in general.

One of the most evident and significant trends in avionics is the move toward higher levels of subsystem integration and functional automation, as discussed in chapter 4. A primary area of advanced avionics system design involves determining the optimal level of integration and the appropriate areas of human-centered functional automation.

Chapter 5 focuses on the great influence that information presentation to pilots has on avionics development, especially in the research labs today. Until recently, avionics developers tried to provide more and more information to pilots without a lot of thought about human workload effects or intuitive information conveyance. It is becoming clear, however, that there is a safety risk when crewmembers become saturated with information and avionics-related tasks. Future avionics will sift, sort, and otherwise help manage the human workload and convey information more intuitively. More avionics design effort is going into providing good flight and systems situation awareness for pilots. Also, to the extent that avionics systems are a cockpit resource for flight crews, effort is going into helping them manage these cockpit resources.

Navigation trends, the subject of chapter 6, have always aimed to increase the number of ways pilots can determine where they are with respect to their intended flight path. We are on the verge of a virtual revolution in navigation capability. With the advent of the satellite-based global positioning system (GPS), the number of navigational systems will decrease at the same time as navigational capability will improve. Likewise, the controversial microwave landing system (MLS) may revolutionize navigational capability in terminal areas.

On the surface it may not seem that there is much to say about the communication trends covered in chapter 7. However, there are clear indications that the digital revolution will encompass communication capability also. Air-ground voice communication will move toward data-link transmission. Other communications, even if voice-type, may include more use of satellite-based systems as opposed to ground-based, line-of-sight direct communication. Also, automated position-reporting communication, which will enhance flight safety by improving collision detection and avoidance, will become more common in the future.

The trends related to flight control have already resulted in significant strides in the transition from analog to digital systems, as shown in chapter 8. With increased sensor developments and digital capability, the flight control trends are headed toward fly-by-wire technology and added capability, such as autoland, envelope protection, stability augmentation, and windshear prediction, detection, and recovery.

In chapter 9 the book culminates with some perspectives on the future of advanced avionics, based on its evolutionary nature. The effects of the Information Age on avionics, as well as the continuing emphasis on integration and automation, are also reviewed.

2. Framework of Avionics Development

2.1. User Acceptance

Aircraft cockpits are being loaded with avionics systems that provide more and more functional capability for flight crews. There are often multiple ways to navigate, communicate, and control the aircraft. Pilots must be able to monitor and use whatever capability the systems offer, and this can lead to problems in pilot training, proficiency, and workload. It is becoming critically important that avionics systems be easy to operate and that information available from these systems be intuitive and easily assimilated. It is unacceptable for users to have to fixate on a control panel or display to relate to it. Pilots are trained to scan the instrument panel continuously and can afford no more than a glance at any one unit at a time. Avionics must first be useful without overtaxing a pilot. It is a real challenge for avionics developers today to build in operational simplicity when adding more and more functional capability. One objective almost seems to preclude the other. Operational simplicity may be a difficult goal to achieve, but it is a worthwhile and necessary goal to meet the user-acceptance test.

Figure 2.1 shows in conceptual form that as system functional capability increases there is a corresponding increase in system operational complexity. One result of this complexity is system-induced pilot error. The goal for user-interface designers is to change the slope of this relationship, as shown in figure 2.1. When the slope is pushed down, then a given level of functional capability will have a correspondingly lower system operational complexity. Likewise, as functional capability increases, the corresponding system operational complexity and associated system-induced human error will increase at a slower rate.

A significant trend in avionics today, especially in the transport category, is to automate many functions. With the powerful technology available, it is tempting for developers to incorporate more automation than is sometimes acceptable to flight crews. An example of today's highly automated systems is an autopilot driven by a flight management system (FMS). Before flight, the pilot enters the flight plan route into the FMS. The FMS has an extensive database that includes navaids, way-points, and SID/STAR (standard instrument departure/standard terminal arrival route) procedures. Using the entered flight plan, inputs from multiple navigation receivers, and the database knowledge of all of the flight plan fixes, the FMS provides steering signals to the autopilot to fly the route automatically. This capability is called lateral nav, or LNAV. The FMS may also have vertical nav (VNAV) capability to fly a preprogrammed altitude profile. In any case, the autopilot can hold an altitude or establish constant climb or descent rates. The pilot's function is to enter the lateral and vertical flight profile into the FMS, couple the FMS to the autopilot, engage the desired autopilot modes, and then monitor the automated system's performance. Many pilots have indicated that this hands-off monitoring leads to boredom and contributes to decreasing pilot proficiency, with obvious ramifications for flight safety.

What many pilots would prefer is that the avionics have the capability to monitor automatically the pilot's hands-on flight performance and provide alerts to the pilot when performance is deviating from acceptable standards. For example, the pilot could enter desired altitude and off-course limits, and the system would signal when a limit is reached. This would permit the flight crews to fly manually if and when they want to and at the same time would facilitate high performance standards. In

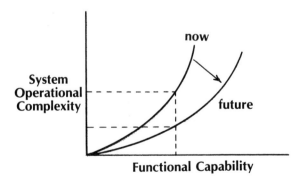

Figure 2.1. Operational complexity versus functional capability

other words, the automation would not preempt the pilot's primary function of total flight responsibility.

There is a real value to using automation for some functions. A natural candidate for preemptive automation is the monitoring function for which a flight engineer is normally responsible. The engine parameters, fluid quantities, pressures, temperatures, flow rates, and the myriad other gauges that the flight engineer in the past has visually monitored can be automatically monitored with data recording of trends and exceedances. This is the purpose of the engine-indicating and crew-alerting system (EICAS) that is located prominently in the center of the instrument panel of modern airliners. Any system parameter that is tending to develop a problem or is approaching a limit can be detected early by automatic means, and the crew can be alerted immediately via messages displayed on the EICAS. When everything is operating normally, the crew is not taxed with this manual monitoring task. Pilot workload is thereby reduced without decreasing basic pilot proficiency. In addition, the "automatic flight engineer" is virtually instantaneous in discovering detrimental system trends and exceedances. This kind of automation has accelerated the trend toward the two-pilot crew in modern airline cockpits.

There are, therefore, times when automation meets with user approval and times when it does not. One clear trend for avionics developers designing new avionics functions and capability is for more awareness of the importance of user acceptance. More about automation is covered in chapter 4.

2.2. Air Traffic Control Environment

An essential part of the framework for future avionics systems is the national airspace system (NAS). The air traffic control (ATC) system is one component of the NAS. Clearly, aircraft avionics must be compatible with ground-based and space-based navigational systems and with ATC communication capability, including datalink communication.

The FAA's national airspace system plan, first conceived in 1981 as a $12-billion modernization program ($16-billion as of 1989), envisions dramatic changes to the ATC system that will have a significant impact on future airborne avionics management systems. For the sake of this discussion, I will use the term flight management system (FMS) to mean the centralized avionics system, since this is the term the FAA uses.

The automated enroute air traffic control program, called the AERA program, was first announced by the FAA in January 1982 as a

$9-billion, third-generation air traffic control program with a long-range goal of completely automating the ATC process by the first decade of the twenty-first century. That is, aircraft on instrument flight plans would be issued computer-determined clearances and conflict-avoidance instructions automatically via the Mode S transponder datalink (see section 7.3). FMS-equipped aircraft will be able to fly direct routes at FMS-determined and ATC-approved fuel-efficient altitudes and speeds. Conflict monitoring will be accomplished by the ATC computer with conflict resolution provided automatically via Mode S to the aircraft involved . The Mode S datalink is a two-way digital communication system that allows the ATC computer to talk directly with the onboard FMS computer to issue, receive, negotiate or resolve, and accept and implement ATC clearances and FMS flight-profile change requests. The obvious implication is that future avionics systems will need to be able to perform in this tightly coupled, automated ATC environment and be compatible with datalink-received ATC directives. At the same time FMSs will need to be able to converse and negotiate with ATC computers for revised clearance requests.

It may seem that the human controller is being taken out of the loop. To a high degree it is true that computers will be automating conflict analysis and planning flight profiles for optimal performance. In the AERA program, the future controller will become more of a system manager and flow analyzer in a strategic sense, rather than a tactical, short-look-ahead traffic separator. With the automated system's knowledge of the total four-dimensional traffic picture (which includes time over fixes), it can plan wide-scale traffic flows. At the same time it ensures traffic separation and facilitates traffic efficiency by planning direct routings and approving onboard FMS fuel-efficient and time-efficient altitude and speed requests to the extent possible. Meanwhile, the pilot will remain in the loop to monitor the computer decisions and communications and can, if appropriate, override the computer and request alternative clearances. It is very likely that the human will continue to participate actively in decision making and approving or changing computer-generated recommendations. Nevertheless, the onboard full-performance FMS will be capable of receiving, analyzing, and proposing alternate actions in a more automated mode. It will also be able to interact with the flight crew via a flight management control and display unit subject to pilot consent or revision. This future control and display unit will include one or more large flat-panel displays with touch-sensitive controls and remote cursor controls.

A brief review of the phased cut-in gives a better feel for the background of AERA. AERA is planned as a three-stage program with the following objectives:

1. To permit aircraft to fly time-efficient and fuel-efficient profiles
2. To increase safety by reducing controller workload and operational errors
3. To increase airspace utilization by integrating enroute flow metering with local and national flow control
4. To increase controller productivity by increasing the number of aircraft and the volume of airspace that a controller team can safely manage

AERA Stage 1. Two major steps are involved in Stage 1. The first is the replacement of the IBM 9020 computers (derivative of the IBM 360, 1964 vintage) in the twenty continental air route traffic control centers (ARTCCs) that provide enroute instrument flight rules (IFR) radar-control coverage for the United States. This was completed in August 1988 and will position the national airspace system for AERA until at least the year 2000. The new IBM 3083/BX1 mainframes have a memory capacity five times larger and a throughput ten times faster. The second step is to automate the air traffic flow-metering process to alleviate congestion caused by weather problems or bunching of flights at major airports. The new computers will regulate flow to avoid in-flight delays as much as possible. The computers will also plan traffic sequencing to expedite arrivals at hubs where traffic convergence causes major congestion. This step should be completed by 1994.

The new ARTCC computers will use flow-control rules and separation standards to generate appropriate clearances, plan altitude changes, detect traffic conflicts and restricted airspace incursions, predict sector workload, and handle intersector handoffs. They will also assist controllers in balancing traffic and prompt controllers with information on planned altitude changes.

Other aspects of Stage 1 originally included the possible phasing-in of the microwave landing system (MLS) to replace the VHF/UHF instrument landing system (ILS) and the phasing-in of new controller terminals to replace old flight-progress strip printers. The FAA refers to these new controller terminals, which are multicolor displays of traffic, weather, and flight data, as sector suite workstations. There will be a total of five thousand of these ARTCC workstations in the FAA's advanced automation system (AAS). The first workstations began a test phase in 1990, with the first operational deliveries scheduled for April 1992. All five thousand stations are to be installed by June 1995. However, a new ATC operational software package is being developed separately and could affect the overall schedule.

AERA Stage 2. It is planned that by the year 2000 Stage 2 will permit pilots to fly direct, off-airway, fuel-efficient flights. The ARTCC computers will probe ahead about twenty minutes in four dimensions to test for collision conflicts and severe weather problems and to propose resolutions. Clearances will be revised from surveillance data to reflect flight-plan deviations. Controllers will still check and revise computer solutions before approving them.

Computer-generated clearances will be sent to aircraft via the digital Mode S transponder datalink, which will largely replace pilot-controller voice communication. The Mode S transponders have selectable addressing capability and provide coverage for major terminals and airspace above 12,500 feet mean sea level (MSL). By the year 2000 coverage will include all airspace above 6,000 MSL as additional Mode S ground systems are added. It is expected that ATC will clear FMS-equipped aircraft to specific fixes for arrival at a designated time (four-dimensional control). By this time in the AERA program, FMSs should be able to automatically datalink waypoint estimated time of arrival (ETA) and performance data back to the ARTCC computers.

A spin-off provided by the Mode S system is the capability to datalink weather information to aircraft upon pilot request, which has another significant implication for FMSs. That is, the FMS would then have available the latest enroute forecasted area winds-aloft and temperature information. This information will permit better performance calculations to optimize flight profiles. Additionally, the ARTCC system will have the capability to reroute traffic automatically around dangerous weather situations.

Another spin-off of Mode S is that the transponders exchange threat data between closing aircraft (traffic-alert and collision-avoidance system, or TCAS, capability is covered in more detail in section 7.6). This data could be processed by the FMS to automatically permit emergency route and altitude deviation for collision avoidance.

AERA Stage 3. Stage 3 is expected to be operational within the first decade of the twenty-first century, but it is contingent on the stabilization of AERA 2. Controllers will no longer have to approve computer decisions, although they will continue to monitor and can override the computers, if desired. Direct routing will be expanded system-wide with fully automatic conflict-monitoring and resolution. I would expect this to be handled largely by direct datalink communication between the ATC computer and the FMS computer, with the controller and pilot acting as observers and interveners when required. The pilot and/or the

FMS will be able to request route and altitude changes, even on a what-if basis, based on new weather and wind data via datalink and get a near-immediate automatic ATC response.

Stage 3 AERA will exploit full four-dimensional capability, with look-ahead nominally forty-five minutes, by automatically being able to handle longer-duration, conflict-free clearances, eventually from takeoff to final approach, or even to what are called Cat 3C landings (category 3C means zero ceiling, zero visibility). The intent is to increase airport and enroute capacity by enhancing arrival sequencing, positive reduced separation, and direct-route flights. By this time FMSs should have the capability of full "airmass" navigation (taking into account winds aloft, pressure gradients, temperature patterns, etc.) and computer-optimized performance. Refer to section 6.6 for a description of futuristic airmass navigation. The result will be maximized fuel economy, in-flight time savings, increased traffic densities, improved efficiency, and increased safety.

Simulation tests conducted by NASA's Ames Research Center have demonstrated the potential payoff from this capability even when some of the aircraft are not FMS-equipped. The tests showed almost no traffic-sequencing delays, as opposed to the frequent controller vectoring required for non-FMS aircraft.

Another result of Stage 3 will be that the current thirty to forty sector positions in each ARTCC will be replaced with four or five region positions with one controller team per region. The twenty ARTCCs and approximately two hundred terminal facilities will be concentrated into a total of only sixty area control facilities.

The futuristic concepts of AERA, especially Stage 3, have not all been accepted with credulity, and therefore whatever capability is designed in to future avionics systems needs to be compatible with the future ATC system. There have been policy disputes between the FAA, pilot groups, airline management, etc., over the concepts and approach of AERA. As an example, the RAND Corporation was commissioned by the FAA to review the FAA AERA plan, and RAND basically characterized some aspects of the plan as unworkable, too costly, and unsafe. For example, the expert-systems software in the ATC computers cannot possibly be 100 percent complete and accurate with respect to situation handling and pattern recognition. RAND also pointed out that because of activity volume and time constraints we cannot rely on human intervention to detect and correct inappropriate computer actions. Controllers who are relegated to the monitoring role may lose optimum alertness and become unable to retain high skill and reaction levels.

RAND proposed a "shared control" alternative, in which primary responsibility for traffic control would remain with human controllers while the automated systems would assist by continuously checking and monitoring their control decisions and proposing alternative plans. In high-traffic periods controllers could turn portions of control activity over to the computer, keeping their workloads relatively constant.

To add a note of practical realism, it should be pointed out that the automated AERA capability will be the result of very complex software. Experience has shown that writing, debugging, and updating complex software is an exceedingly difficult task, with associated risks and likelihood of error.

2.3. Technology Factors

2.3.1. System-level Technology

Displays. In the barnstorming days of the 1930s, aircraft instrumentation consisted of dials and gauges. It was not until the 1950s that complex, integrated electromechanical displays such as the horizontal situation indicator (HSI) became available. The HSI presents navigation deviation from a preselected course superimposed with gyro heading information. This instrument was a breakthrough in cockpit displays and helped the pilot become oriented with respect to the desired flight track.

Other electromechanical displays existed in this period, notably artificial horizons that included complex gearing, meter movements, and servos. In the 1960s television cathode ray tubes (CRTs) and transistor technology evolved to the point where they were introduced into aircraft cockpits as part of monochrome weather radar displays. By 1978 rugged, color shadow-mask CRTs had been introduced as part of the electronic flight instrument system (EFIS) for use in the Boeing 757 and 767 airliners. EFIS consists of primary flight, navigation, and engine and warning displays.

The most readily apparent effect of technological advances in modern cockpits is the preponderance of CRT displays instead of the myriad of electromechanical displays. The decade of the 1980s saw EFIS CRTs become firmly accepted in modern airline cockpits. The color capability adds a lot to the readability of the flight information presentation. With CRTs information can be removed when it is not needed. This improves the readability of the information that is displayed. Likewise, flags and alerts, active modes, and other information may come and go from the displays, as appropriate. In addition to this kind of symbology and format versatility, CRTs have greater reliability than electromechanical displays. Better reliability is largely the result of the elimination of moving mechanical parts. The versatility of EFIS is a great advantage because fewer units can display all of the information required by activating electronic symbology automatically when appropriate and by permitting the menu selection of various formats, as desired. This reduces cockpit clutter and decreases workload since only the desired information is displayed and unnecessary information is totally removed from view, making for a cleaner, easier to understand, and more intuitive instrument panel. This can make it easier to add more display information without adding clutter since the same unit may be used and an additional separate display format can be selected.

Now that display formats and symbology are controllable, the current trend in display technology is toward flat-panel technology to eliminate the long CRT neck and reduce the weight, power consumption, and heat dissipation of CRTs. Flat-panel display technology generally consists of individually addressable pixels. Eight-by-eight-inch displays have on the order of one million pixels. For color displays one-third of the pixels are red, one-third are blue, and one-third are green. Various symbology and color shades are created by electronically turning on the required pixels, which are addressed via a row-and-column matrix arrangement. Solid-state flat panels also have much better reliability than high-power CRT displays, and high-resolution flat panels have excellent readability.

Several different flat-panel technologies exist — LCD (liquid crystal display), EL (electroluminescent), and plasma, to name the more common avionics-application contenders. The active-matrix LCD (AM-LCD) flat panel is the most promising display technology for near-term use in aircraft. The principal attributes of LCD technology are low cost, low power consumption, low weight, and ruggedness. Some of the LCD attributes still needing improvement are manufacturability, screen size, temperature range, dynamic brightness range, resolution, contrast, gray scale, viewing angle, and color capability (Perry and Wallich 1985, 65). Among flat-panel displays, LCDs are said to have the inside track. As Allan R. Kmetz (1987, 24) says, "Supertwist LCD's are cheaper by about a factor of two than plasma and EL, partly because the latter require high-voltage IC's which will always be more expensive, and LCD's have the unique advantage of truly low power consumption." Meanwhile, CRTs measuring up to eight inches square continue to dominate displays with high brightness and resolution.

In addition to the introduction of a monochrome active-matrix LCD flat-panel display as part of a datalink system in 1988, the first widespread use of flat-panel avionics displays was with some new TCAS units introduced in 1989. Advances in active-matrix LCDs promise to solve some of the LCD problems related to speed, contrast, viewing angle, and simplicity of control.

For many years the military has favored thin-film electroluminescent (TFEL) technology because of its wide operating temperatures, ruggedness, and quality. Because of the military's interest, EL technology should continue to progress. EL displays are fully solid-state; moreover, they do not have the viewing angle problems of LCDs, have better resolution, and have potential for lower power consumption than do LCDs.

For avionics display applications, plasma technology seems to be the least promising of the major contenders because it lacks color potential, sufficient resolution, and gray scale. Table 2.1 summarizes the attributes of each of the major display technologies.

Table 2.1. Attributes of major display technologies

	CRT	EL	AM-LCD[a]	Plasma
Power consumption	fair	fair-good	good	fair
Screen size	excellent	fair	fair	good-excellent
Weight	poor	excellent	excellent	excellent
Ruggedness	fair-good	good-excellent	excellent	excellent
Temperature range	good	excellent	fair-good	excellent
Brightness	excellent	good-excellent	excellent	good
Resolution	good-excellent	good	fair-good	good
Contrast	good-excellent	good	excellent	good
Gray scale	excellent	fair	poor	poor
Viewing angle	good	good	excellent	good-excellent
Color capability	excellent	good	excellent	fair
Cost	low	medium-high	high	medium
Manufacturability	excellent	fair	poor	good
Reliability	poor	fair	fair	good

Sources: Perry, Tekla S., and Paul Wallich, "Computer Displays: New Choices, New Tradeoffs," *IEEE Spectrum* (July 1985): 65; Williams, Tom, "Flat-Panel Displays Come on Strong in Speed, Resolution and Color," *Computer Design* (Feb. 1, 1989): 79.
[a]Active matrix LCD

Bus Architecture. Advanced avionics systems are predominantly, if not totally, digital in nature. A recurring theme throughout these chapters is the trend toward higher levels of system integration. The digital data bus is one of the things necessary to make integration possible. Virtually all modern avionics units are computer based and are interconnected via digital buses. Standardized data-transmission protocols exist to facilitate the compatibility of a wide variety of avionics units with each other. The MIL-STD-1553B multiplex bus is very common for the military. For commercial avionics, the Aeronautical Radio, Inc., (ARINC) 429 digital bus is common. The digital bus architecture for avionics systems is well entrenched and will continue to proliferate.

The 1553 multiplex bus is a 1-Mbps (megabit per second), bidirectional, time-division multiplex data-transfer bus that was first conceived in 1968 by the military and industry to reduce the wire count and associated weight problems of complex avionics systems. The current version, MIL-STD-1553B, was inaugurated in 1978. A bus controller commands each data transfer by specifying the sending unit and the receiving unit for each transaction. Typically, this bus is implemented with redundant bus cables and redundant bus controllers to enhance fail-passive and fail-operational capability.

The next-generation 1553 bus is designated as MIL-STD-1773 and replaces bus wires with fiber-optic cables. The protocol is the same as that of the MIL-STD-1553B. Although the data rate is also the same, it may be possible to implement a version that is capable of 50 Mbps. This will be highly desirable as avionics systems evolve to include data-intensive capability such as high-resolution digital maps that require wide bandwidth. Other advantages of an optical bus include lighter weight; immunity from electromagnetic interference, pulse radiation, and lightning; and less signal attenuation, which allows much longer cable runs.

The ARINC 429 digital bus has been around since the mid-1960s and is the standard avionics bus in civil aircraft. Unlike the MIL-STD-1553B bus, the ARINC 429 bus is a unidirectional bus with one sending unit transmitting to one or more receiving units. Each unit that must distribute data to other units must do so on separate ARINC 429 buses, increasing the number of wires and adding interface circuitry weight. The MIL-STD-1553B bus avoids these drawbacks. The 429 bus is also much slower than the 1553, operating at one of two speeds, 12 to 14.5 kHz or 100 kHz. However, it has served the advancement of commercial digital avionics very well. With interface standardization between various avionics units, higher levels of integration and data correlation have been made possible within the limits of the one-way bus architecture.

A replacement for the 429 bus is being developed, originally spearheaded by the Boeing Airplane Company to facilitate the inclusion of advanced avionics in future airliners. Designated as the ARINC 629 bus, it is similar to the 1553 bus. It is a two-way broadcast bus that permits any unit to communicate with any other unit on the bus, but it does not require a bus controller. A unique aspect is the scheme by which each unit listens for bus activity and waits for bus availability. A special protocol was developed to avoid access collisions while still ensuring priority data flow. The data transfer rate is 2 megabits per second over a bus that may be either wire or optical fiber. In keeping with the trend toward increasing integration, the 629 bus can integrate up to 120 units, as opposed to 32 for 1553 and 20 for 429.

The military is in the process of developing and evaluating a high-speed broadcast avionics data bus with a token-passing protocol (no central bus controller) that operates at 50 Mbps. This represents the state of the art in avionics bus architectures. As systems become more and more integrated, the need to exchange information among system components is increasing. This exchange takes place over the system bus, which at some point can become congested with information, especially when the information is highly data-intensive, such as video data or real-time flight control data. The 50-Mbps per second fiber-optic bus was developed under the U.S. Air Force Pave Pillar program. Up to sixty-four system components may be interconnected up to three hundred feet apart with high data-exchange capability and minimum message-delay latency.

Other buses have been developed for computer networks, and some of these could be incorporated into avionics systems in the 1990s. One such bus is called Fiber Distributed Data Interface (FDDI), which is a 100-Mbps fiber-optic bus. This very high speed bus lends itself to future avionics capability that involves high data-transfer quantities and rates such as those used for graphics. Fiber-optic buses weigh much less than wire buses; moreover, they have high immunity to electromagnetic interference, have a low bit-error rate, do not radiate, and do not have the grounding problems associated with wire buses. FDDI will permit integration of up to five hundred units, but bus-attachment is more difficult than it is for wire buses.

Open Systems Approach. Recent advances in system-level technology include a desire for a more organized and standardized approach for data transfer and subsystem interoperability. Open systems interconnection (OSI) is a seven-layer software protocol to facilitate information exchange between communication networks. The need for this information exchange grew out of the proliferation of wide-area data-processing networks and the need for information exchange between these networks. OSI was adopted in 1984 by the International Standards Organization (ISO). By the late 1980s avionics developers were beginning to employ OSI as a means to permit efficient information exchange between onboard systems and ground data networks. The first applications were associated with the aircraft communcations, addressing, and reporting system (ACARS) datalink and the onboard maintenance system (OMS) for maintenance-related information. New electronic library systems (ELS) are also employing OSI for general information exchange. This exchange of information involves the digital datalink capability.

OSI is one aspect of the "open architecture" concept that gained the attention of the avionics world in the early 1990s. The open-architecture concept makes use of industry-standard parts, buses, software languages, software packages, protocols, etc. Making use of standards in all of these areas maximizes the compatibility and interoperability of the associated interfaces. This obviates the need for designing custom hardware and software from scratch. More importantly, as technology advances rapidly, new and improved hardware and software modules can replace older versions through relatively simple insertions because the interfaces are standard. That is, the hardware pieces and software modules are plug-in compatible with the system, ensuring interoperability.

System-level Packaging. An avionics system is made up of functional subsystems, such as communication radios, navigation receivers, flight control computers, etc. Traditionally, these units have been separate "black boxes." As a result of the trend toward subsystem integration, it will become more common for these units to be packaged as card modules for plug-in to a rack. Rather than line-replaceable units (LRUs), these are known as line-replaceable modules (LRMs). Section 3.1.4 describes the integrated communication, navigation, identification avionics (ICNIA) program, which involves standard form-factor common modules, integrated rack configuration, module reconfiguration, and resource sharing. Section 3.1.1 covers the Pave Pillar program, another modular avionics architecture program. These concepts are a part of the trend in avionics packaging. Industry standards such as ARINC 651 are being developed to outline the guidelines for modular avionics packaging. Functional modularity facilitates automatic reconfiguration of modules and built-in test capability to the LRM level for easy fault isolation and replacement. This permits higher system reliability and better aircraft availability.

2.3.2. Device-level Technology

Digital Technology. Much of the success of modern avionics can be attributed to the revolution in digital technology over the last twenty years. After the 1947 invention of the silicon transistor, solid-state technology developed rather slowly until 1959, when the introduction of the silicon integrated circuit (IC) sparked an explosion of digital development. It heralded the transition from analog to digital technology and ever-higher on-chip densities. In 1970 large-scale integration (LSI) was achieved, and shortly afterward, in 1971, the first microprocessor appeared, the Intel 4004, which had a computing power equivalent to the ENIAC, the first fully electronic digital computer built in 1946. In 1976, only five years after the Intel 4004, the Cray-1 supercomputer appeared. Personal desktop computers became available only one year later in 1977. By 1980 very large scale integration (VLSI) was introduced along with the first 32-bit microprocessor. The technological advances are continuing today. The 1986 breakthrough in superconductors could conceivably lead to further developments in supercomputers. For example, superconducting electronic circuitry promises superhigh data-transmission rates that will permit more efficient datalink capability. Henderson (1991, 66) indicates that superconductivity and optical transmission have a long-term potential for petaFLOPS (10^{15} floating-point operations per second) computing speeds.

Although silicon-based integrated circuits have long been the mainstay, GaAs (gallium arsenide) devices have great potential to outdo silicon. GaAs transistor research dates back to the 1960s, and today's GaAs devices show a four-to-one performance advantage over silicon. In terms of speed, the long-favored emitter-coupled logic (ECL) may be displaced by GaAs technology, especially for application as microwave and millimeter-wave devices. Circuit density, too, is an attribute of GaAs and gives it the capability of placing up to 100,000 gates into one device with manufacturing yields that rival ECL. In price, future GaAs devices are projected to be 30 to 40 percent less costly than silicon ECL (Dugan 1989). Jeffrey Rowe (1990, 32) indicates that "Overall, GaAs integrated circuits (ICs) switch at faster rates, pass signals faster, exhibit lower noise, consume less power at high speeds (up to four times the speed at less than half the power of comparable silicon devices), operate over a wider temperature range and are inherently more radiation hardened than silicon ICs." He continues, "On the down side, GaAs is not as abundant and is much more expensive than silicon, and development has been impeded by the difficulties in obtaining defect-free wafers greater than four inches in diameter." Nevertheless, silicon has a continuing legacy, and "experts estimate that dynamic memories of 256 M-bits in planar technology will be achieved in the 1990s. (As a comparison, note that in early 1992 IBM released an advanced hard disk drive with a 1-gigabit magnetic memory capacity in a one-square-inch space.) Another estimate indicates that "devices on a logic IC may rise toward 100 million by the year 2000" (Gelsinger et al. 1989, 46).

Another contributing factor to increase processor speeds is reduced instruction set computer (RISC) technology. The objective of RISC processors is to streamline the rich set of internal instructions that tend to slow down a CPU. This results in lower on-chip transistor counts and a much faster throughput. For example, Intel's non-RISC 80386 processor contains 275,000 transistors, while Sun's RISC-based SPARC contains only 50,000 transistors and has twice the processing speed. RISC technology tends to be advantageous for register-intensive computational applications, such as graphics engines that perform frequently repeated operations. However, the conventional CISC (complex instruction set computer) will probably continue to be favored for embedded, multitasking, and real-time processing, primarily because a typical algorithm for a RISC CPU can require up to 50 percent more code. This additional memory requirement for many applications can be a system-level, real-estate, and cost problem.

Texas Instruments has demonstrated a 32-bit 12,900-gate GaAs RISC processor that runs at a 100-MHz clock rate. This is one of the largest functional blocks built on a GaAs substrate, though 200-MHz devices will be available in the near term. A GaAs-based supercomputer currently being developed uses 32-bit, 0.8-micron technology with a throughput capability of 217 million FLOPS. Each processor device contains 45,000 gates. This supercomputer is planned to support the ATF and NASP development projects (see section 3.2). Processors with the capability of one trillion operations per second may be available as early as 1995. It is estimated that RISC processors will soon account for at least 25 percent of the 32-bit device market. For the future, it is likely that combination RISC/CISC processors will evolve in which the RISC section of the CPU will serve as the core processor, augmented with a CISC section tailored to specific applications.

While 8-bit microprocessors are becoming obsolete and 16-bit devices are becoming the current mainstay, 32-bit units are readily available and are being incorporated into current avionics designs. In February 1989 Intel announced the first 64-bit microprocessor. It contains over one million transistors, compared with 275,000 for the previous-generation Intel 80386 microprocessor. This microprocessor, designated the 80860, continues the trend of integrating more and more capability at the on-chip level. For example, Intel has integrated into the 80860 large caches for instructions and data, specialized circuitry for floating-point calculations with the capability of 80 million floating-point operations per second, and graphics capability of 16 million 16-bit picture elements per second. This device is RISC-based for better speed (up to 120 million operations per second) and runs at 40 MHz. A measure of its power is its benchmark of 90,000 dhrystones, as compared with 13,000 dhrystones for the predecessor 80386. The overall performance of the 80860 is estimated at about half that of a Cray-1 supercomputer. The trend toward larger CPUs continues. Motorola introduced its 32-bit 68040 microprocessor in 1989, and it, too, contained over one million transistors. With current research advances in IC lithography, micro-miniature interconnect technology, and dielectrics, laboratory achievements of 0.1 micron devices and devices with over ten million transistors on a chip have been obtained.

According to Intel executives (Gelsinger et al. 1989), the microprocessor of the year 2000 will have, hypothetically, the following attributes:

One-square-inch die size
Fifty million transistors
Four parallel processors
Aggregate performance of over 2,000 million instructions per second (MIPS)
250-MHz operating speed
Operating voltage as low as 2.5 volts
64-bit addressing and data capability
Peak of one billion floating-point operations per second for each of two vector units
Cache space of two megabytes

At the rate that microprocessors have grown since their inception, it is not unimaginable to expect computer mainframe capability out of future microprocessors by the turn of the century. Likewise, by the year 2000, memory and logic devices will likely be exceeding 100 million transistors in density.

Artificial intelligence applications involving neural networks are on the horizon. Neural networks are large arrays of processors on a chip operating in parallel to perform complex high-speed operations such as pattern recognition. According to John Joss (1987, 71), they are "a new computer metaphor that should bring a major contribution to cockpit technology in the 1990s."

Some of the impetus for the microminiaturization of devices came from the very high speed integrated circuit (VHSIC) program originally formulated by the U.S. Department of Defense in 1978. The purpose of this program is for the device industry to develop advanced, next-generation, very large scale integration (VLSI) devices to be used in military systems. The goals for these superminiature devices include increased speed, reduced power consumption, radiation hardening, improved reliability and maintainability, and extensive device-level built-in test capability. The built-in test capability is one of the major aspects of the VHSIC program. The devices have self-contained spare circuits with fault detection capability to bypass failed devices for self-repair. Phase 1 of the VHSIC program ran from March 1981 until the delivery of 25-MHz devices with internal trace widths of 1.25 microns in 1985. Comparatively, prior to the VHSIC program, the trace width for high-density devices was typically 4 to 7 microns, having decreased from 20 microns in the early 1970s. The drive to decrease trace widths is aimed at permitting high-density packaging for shorter internal circuit runs. With these shorter runs, propagation times decrease. Phase 2 began in October 1984 with the goal of producing 100-MHz 0.5 micron devices.

The military is especially interested in fostering this program because high-density, high-speed devices are particularly useful in military applications such as real-time intensive image processing (target recognition, for example). The Department of Defense (DOD) spent more than $1 billion in the first seven years of the program and the work continues. James Rawles (1989, 70) has made a prediction: "By 1995, we'll see production of 0.25-micron chips and a [technology] generation later, 0.10-micron chips." The processing speed of some VHSIC devices is noteworthy: "In June 1988, IBM delivered the first all-VHSIC common signal processor (CSP) to the U.S. Air Force. According to a company announcement, the CSP, which is packaged in a 1-cubic-foot box, will be able to perform 1.8 billion floating point operations per second or 7.2 billion fixed point operations per second" (Rawles 1989, 72). VHSIC devices are beginning to be used in new military development programs, but these programs will not be fielded until the mid-1990s. The value of the VHSIC program cannot be estimated until the results of VHSIC-based systems are known.

Packaging. Since the advent of the transistor, circuit densities have increased by six orders of magnitude. However, until recently, the packaging for these subminiature circuits has not received a lot of attention. Even the latest superdense ICs, including the U.S. government's VHSIC and the MIMIC (microwave/millimeter-wave monolithic integrated circuit), have not concentrated on the potential of the latest packaging techniques. The longtime standard dual-inline package (DIP) is approaching its waning years and is beginning to be replaced with new packaging techniques. The trends in electronic packaging are being forged by the need for smaller-sized equipment, higher reliability, faster computing, lighter weight, lower manufacturing costs, and improved functional performance.

Digital technology has evolved from discrete devices to VLSI, including programmable logic arrays (PLAs), gate arrays, and application-specific ICs (ASICs). The goal has been to consolidate multiple functions within fewer devices for the reasons indicated above. However, more dense devices have resulted in higher heat dissipation and high pin counts. With pin counts of up to five hundred, package size is necessarily increased with resulting higher insertion force and potential contact problems. As the microcircuit logic-gate switching speed has increased, the major source of electrical delays has transferred over to interdevice connections. Thus, the thrust to increase circuit density within a device is continuing so that the connections between chips are reduced. Surface-mount technology (SMT) provides a solution to increase chip-circuit density, thereby increasing reliability and circuit speed. It is estimated that SMT can result in a six-to-one reduction in volume, a four-to-one reduction in weight (Poradish 1988, 9), and a five-to-one improvement in reliability (Giordano 1988, 1). Since electrical delays attributable to packaging can account for more than 50 percent of the total system delay, use of SMT can significantly reduce these delays. Side benefits include manufacturing economy (autoassembly), smaller overall circuit size, lower overall weight, improved thermal management, and improved functional performance. Other benefits include reduced parasitic coupling (therefore, higher operating frequencies) and lower electro-magnetic interference (EMI) emissions, less noise, and lower resistive losses.

The future will probably see increasing usage of multichip modules that will contain conventional silicon chips, GaAs devices (for lower noise and higher speed), and SMT packages on a single large substrate. More vertically stacked substrates will come into use to shorten interconnections, increase propagation speeds, and generally make electronics more compact. These attributes are of considerable importance to avionics because weight, size, power consumption, and functional performance are premium commodities on aircraft. Device heat-piping and liquid-cooled cold plates will also be used to cool the avionics devices. This will decrease the reliance on aircraft cooling systems and thus decrease power consumption and weight. Multichip modules permit the integration of as many as one hundred complex VLSI chips interconnected on a single silicon wafer. Walter Schroen (1988, 140) anticipates the following changes: "Ultimately, custom substrates perhaps constructed from aluminum nitride or silicon carbide may be used as mini-circuit boards that interconnect through silicon racks. The entire assembly may be soldered together in a single step, replacing many of the card racks now common in electronic equipment." The use of SMT "could make it possible, within a decade or two, to produce airliner avionics mounted entirely in the panel, requiring no external cooling equipment" (Giordano 1988, 3).

Device-level trends include the continuation of device miniaturization, the on-chip integration of functional circuitry, and more extensive circuit-level fault-detection capability for automatic removal of faulty circuitry and the cut-in of standby on-chip replacement circuitry. The overall result will be smaller, faster, more functional, more powerful, and more reliable avionics units.

2.3.3. Software Technology

Software technology has become a very hot issue of concern for avionics development in recent years. With the advent of electronic flight displays (glass cockpit) and computer-based, processing-intensive avionics units, software — rather than hardware — has become "the way" to implement avionics functions. Today, it is generally estimated that up to 90 percent of an avionics development project is software oriented. The remaining percentage involves the hardware associated with the system CPU, memory, and subsystem interfacing circuitry. With the basic simplicity of an embedded microcomputer architecture and the decreasing costs of peripheral ICs, project cost emphasis is shifting to the software side of the equation. As software handles more and more of the system functionality, it becomes more complex, and this contributes to increasing software effort and cost. In the past, avionics software effort was on the simple side, small and low-cost, typically involving a single programmer using assembly language. Now, the software effort is more frequently on the complex side, large and high-cost, typically involving teams of programmers using high-order languages.

Some sources feel that we are in a software crisis related to a surge of massive real-time embedded projects for which industry has neither the necessary depth of experience nor adequate knowledge and skill. The way out of the software crunch involves the embracing of software engineering goals and principles that have been known for over twenty years but, until recently, have remained largely in the background, more academic endeavor than practical necessity.

In 1974 the Department of Defense realized software costs were increasing rapidly for embedded computer systems such as avionics equipment. It was evident that software language standardization was desirable to contain development costs and to increase productivity. The existing languages were reviewed to determine whether any could serve as a universal standard. None met all of the desired attributes. So in 1975 the effort began in earnest to document requirements for a new language. A design competition concluded in May 1979 with Cii-Honeywell Bull winning a contract to develop a new language, which was given the name Ada. (The DOD named the language for Augusta Ada Byron [1815–1852], daughter of Lord Byron, who is credited with "programming" Charles Babbage's mechanical computational machine. Ada is a registered trademark of the U.S. Government Ada Joint Program Office.) After a major review of the completed language, the American

National Standards Institute (ANSI) published their Language Reference Manual (LRM) in January 1983, signaling acceptance of Ada as a viable standard. Effort then began to develop an Ada programming-support environment consisting of standard software development tools. This support environment is a key to a particular language's effectiveness. As the Ada support environment matures, the effectiveness of Ada will heighten.

These efforts to establish a universal language were aimed not just at eliminating the proliferation of expensive languages and their assorted tools but also at moving toward what has become known as software engineering. A primary goal of software engineering is that software source code should be developed in a modular way. Then software modules can be "hooked up" in various ways to implement new functions, just as hardware modules can be connected. This minimizes the frequent reinvention of software routines. Software modules can be developed that accept specific input and generate resultant output. So long as the input requirements are met, it is no longer necessary to take the time and expense to design or understand how the module performs its function. The module operates on the input and generates an output with a known format that can be used as input to the next module. This concept is well established for hardware development and minimizes the associated expenses. Likewise, the software engineering principle of software modularity promises to minimize development costs during the design of new software-based systems.

In a classic paper, Douglas Ross, John Goodenough, and C. A. Irvine (1975) consolidated the goals and principles of software engineering:

Understandability. The program's conceptual structure and implementation are clear.
Modifiability. The program may be changed in a controlled way.
Reliability. The program consistently does what the programmer wants it to do.
Efficiency. The program operates in a timely manner.

For a given program, these goals must be balanced to meet the program requirements. The authors went on to detail software engineering principles, which are intended to help achieve the goals:

Modularity. Highly independent subunits with well-defined interfaces
Localization. Related modules located close to each other
Abstraction. Hierarchy of levels, with highest-level modules dealing

in abstraction and lowest-level modules dealing in implementation details

Information hiding. Details of a module visible only to other modules that need the visibility

Uniformity. Consistent and nonconfusing notation and terminology

Completeness. No essentials omitted

Confirmability. Testability to ensure that program requirements are met and that errors are detectable

In addition to these principles spelled out by the authors, other considerations have evolved in the continuing process of improving software. Some of these are program *portability* from one host or target processor to another and *robustness* of code, which is the code's ability to recover from unexpected situations that otherwise might cause a software system to crash.

Just as the trends in software languages moved from machine code to assembly code to higher-order languages, the trend in the high-order languages is to employ the principles of software engineering to a greater extent.

Significant functional capability can be designed efficiently in software that, in turn, runs in an embedded processing system to drive other avionics systems and displays. During the design and development phases, software can be changed and enhanced, avoiding hardware redesign and again minimizing costs. This minimization is achieved primarily by increasing the development team's efficiency. That is, the time to encode any changes and validate the results is reduced, and better results are obtained. Product validation/verification and customer acceptance are then achieved more efficiently and with a higher confidence level.

Ada is still a relatively new language. Although it was designed to take advantage of lessons learned from previous languages and to incorporate the principles of software engineering, no doubt we will encounter reasons to develop future languages that facilitate the software development process even better.

There are various methods existing to develop software in a modular way. The top-down decomposition method begins by dividing the overall problem into pieces and then subdividing these pieces, and so on, until each low-level piece becomes a simple subprogram to code. Object-oriented design starts by modeling the overall problem in terms of the objects that are to be manipulated and the operations that are to be performed on the objects. Modules are then developed using the objects as focal points. These modules will consist of subprograms that focus on the object operations. Various techniques now exist to develop software, and new techniques will evolve to employ the goals and principles of software engineering in the continuing process of making software development more predictable, efficient, and cost-effective.

A relatively new development in software engineering is called computer-aided software engineering (CASE). CASE involves a set of computer tools that help make software development more efficient. These tools support design and project management, coding and debugging, simulation and testing, maintenance, and documentation. The trend toward using CASE should result in a more efficient and effective software development effort. Another new development in software development is a higher consciousness for software quality that involves more effective in-process reviews and code walk-throughs, requirements compliance, configuration tracking, and software verification and testing. At the same time, software development for the long term will move in the direction of more automatic code generation and documentation. These advances in software-related technology play an important role in advanced avionics programs.

2.3.4. Expert Systems and Artificial Intelligence

Expert systems (ES) are distinguished from artificial intelligence (AI) by the AI system's ability to learn from and/or use past sensory experience and its ability to use this knowledge in decision making. ES capability is basically a set of fixed rules developed from knowledge of human experts. Although knowledge-based expert systems and artificial intelligence have been around for several years, they have not been widely used in avionics. They find application in image-recognition and speech-recognition systems, natural-language systems, and handwriting analysis, all of which could find eventual application in commercial avionics systems. There is, however, potential to employ basic ES/AI principles in the near term in at least two avionics processing areas: diagnostic maintenance and situation analysis. An ES algorithm could handle a flight diversion in an emergency situation. On the surface this is a simple arithmetic problem that can be handled easily by a flight management system. The FMS has knowledge of wind data, fuel status, and airports and can determine the best airport to divert to in the least time.

However, other considerations could be added, such as destination ceiling, visibility, approach minimums, medical facilities, rescue capability, runway weight capability, forecast weather, aircraft altitude capability, company preferences, NOTAMs (notices to airmen), etc. The airline captain must weigh all of these factors logically when making a decision.

A knowledge-based AI system goes through an IF-AND/OR-THEN process involving numerous decision branches in the same way that the captain would.

In general terms, ES takes advantage of human expert knowledge and experience in a system that automatically analyzes situations and makes logical decisions more quickly and accurately than the average human can. This decision making involves a forward-chaining, rule-based inference engine to deal with known facts and "fuzzy truths" compared with a knowledge and experience database to select the most probable conclusions. The inference engine mechanism traces multiple decision paths in an allotted time period, pruning lower confidence paths as it goes. This capability assists the human decision maker by fusing and interpreting massive amounts of sensory inputs that otherwise would cause overload.

The thing that separates ES from normal logic processing is that ES involves massive iterative IF-THEN decisions derived from highly interrelated factors. For example, system troubleshooting depends largely on the experienced technician's evaluating several symptoms and using knowledge of the system operation to develop judgments on likely fault sources. The technician might mentally follow several tree branches in the fault search, come to a dead end, back up and follow a different branch, and repeat this process many times before finding the actual fault source. ES can emulate this thought process very quickly according to logic rules designed by a human expert. This capability is particularly valuable, for example, in a military combat environment to evaluate weapon lethality and develop an attack plan. Likewise, commercial avionics could apply ES principles to advantage to increase flight safety and improve flight crew effectiveness.

Intelligent actions in the cockpit depend on the ability of the pilot to acquire all the information possible, analyze the data accurately, and come to valid conclusions very quickly. ES emulates this human-expert data processing. In avionics, ES is particularly useful in a single-pilot military aircraft during combat operations to analyze massive data related to known friendly information and unknown enemy operations. The proliferation of sensors and the information made available by modern electronic surveillance measures (ESM) systems would overwhelm the pilot with information if it were not for automatic processing such as ES and AI. Both ES and AI relieve the pilot from much of the mental processing, but the automatic system still maintains human expert decison making through use of ES and AI.

Note, however, that to be effective in avionics functions, especially critical functions, the ES rules must be accurate and 100 percent complete. Present expert systems do not learn, and they do not make assumptions they were not told to make.

Developing an ES system can be difficult in that it depends so largely on extracting complete knowledge from an expert. In many cases, experts cannot articulate what they know or why they draw the conclusions they do. If the ES rule base is incomplete, invalid conclusions could result. Therefore, ES applications in the avionics flight control or flight management areas must be debugged thoroughly.

Typical commercial rule-based ES and AI systems are written in PROLOG and LISP and other languages optimized for ES and AI, and they use large memories (millions of words), with processing on the order of one million instructions per second (MIPS). Avionics applications may be limited to much less memory while requiring much higher processing speed to generate decisions in a fraction of a second. Searching rule bases is inherently time-consuming, making real-time operation very difficult. Nevertheless, successful ES and AI development has been demonstrated using the limited capability of the MIL-STD-1750A instruction set with 64K of 16-bit words, written in Ada and operating at 1 MIPS. However, large-scale avionics ES and AI systems differ from typical applications (e.g., manufacturing, robotics, etc.) in terms of problem dynamics, response-time constraints, user-interface requirements, and the continuous technology advances. The extensive processing resources required for ES and AI raises questions about compatibility with existing avionics architectures. Note that expert systems are symbolic programs by nature, and most computers are optimized for numeric processing. However, hardware support is becoming available for ES and AI applications. In 1987 Texas Instruments began marketing a 550,000-transistor, 32-bit microprocessor with onboard LISP that is intended to increase the speed and flexibility of AI systems. The bottom line, however, is that useful avionics ES and AI applications are dependent on very good problem modeling and on establishing accurate boundaries for the embedded knowledge base.

Generally, in future avionics ES and AI will be incorporated to perform the following functions:

System fault diagnostics
Emergency recognition and response
Speech recognition
Embedded help function to resolve operational questions
Collision-avoidance response
System reconfiguration for fault tolerance and graceful degradation
Bounding performance ranges to improve FMS response time

2.3.5. Advanced Technological Areas

Identifying specific technologies that affect avionics trends and following advancements in these technologies are important to understanding the avionics trends. The Pentagon has a critical technologies plan that identifies technologies thought to be critical to maintaining leading-edge defense systems. This plan, a list of twenty-two technologies and their objectives, is reproduced in table 2.2.

Most of these government technology priorities have an association with avionics applications, and avionics will benefit from advances in these areas. The spin-offs from these government thrusts will come via NASA and military research programs and from government contracts given to university researchers.

2.4. Political and Regulatory Aspects

By *political aspects* I refer to political action (possibly resulting from public pressures) and governmental action that have a bearing on both the national airspace system (NAS) and onboard avionics that must be compatible with the NAS.

In the United States, the Federal Aviation Administration, whose administrator reports to the secretary of transportation, has the authority to regulate air commerce. It operates the air traffic control and air navigation systems and is responsible for certifying avionics equipment. It also approves ground-based and space-based systems for aeronautical applications. Generally, the FAA establishes and enforces safety regulations for all aspects of civil aviation. Within the FAA, the following divisions (*Washington Information Directory 1987–1988* [hereafter *WID*], 588 ff.) influence the incremental evolution of avionics.

AVIATION POLICY AND PLANS (part of Policy and International Aviation Affairs): responsible for economic and regulatory policy for domestic aviation

INTERNATIONAL AVIATION (part of Policy and International Aviation Affairs): formulates policy in regard to international civil aviation

AIR TRAFFIC: operates the national air traffic control system

AIRWORTHINESS (part of Aviation Standards): approves designs and specifications for avionics

PROGRAM ENGINEERING AND MAINTENANCE SERVICE (part of Development and Logistics): designs, develops, purchases, and operates technical equipment for ATC and navigation

Table 2.2. Pentagon critical technologies plan

Critical technology	Objectives
1. Microelectronic circuits fabrication	Production of ultrasmall integrated electronic devices for high-speed computers, sensitive receivers, automatic controls, etc.
2. Gallium arsenide (GaAs) and other compound semiconductors	Preparation of high-purity GaAs and other compound semiconductor substrates and their films for microelectronic substrates
3. Software producibility	Generation of affordable and reliable software in timely fashion
4. Parallel computer architectures	Ultrahigh-speed computing by simultaneous use of all processing capabilities in the next generation of computers
5. Machine intelligence and robotics	Incorporation of human "intelligence" and actions into mechanical devices
6. Simulation and modeling	Testing of concepts and designs without building physical replicas
7. Integrated optics	Optical memories and optical signal and data processing
8. Fiber optics	Ultralow-loss fibers and optical components such as switches, couplers, and multiplexers for communications, navigation, etc.
9. Sensitive radars	Radar sensors capable of detecting low-observable targets and/or capable of noncooperative target classification, recognition, and/or identification
10. Passive sensors	Sensors not needing to emit signals (hence passive) to detect targets, monitor the environment, or determine the status or condition of equipment.
11. Automatic target recognition	Combination of computer architecture, algorithms, and signal processing for near-real-time automation of detection, classification, and tracking of targets
12. Phased arrays	Formation of spatial beams by controlling the phase and amplitude of RF signals at individual sensor elements distributed along an array (radar, underwater acoustic, or other)
13. Data fusion	Machine integration and/or interpretation of data and their presentation in a form convenient to the human operator
14. Signature control	Ability to control the target signature (radar, optical, acoustic, or other) and thereby enhance the survivability of vehicles and weapon systems
15. Computational fluid dynamics	Modeling of complex fluid flow to make dependable predictions by computing, thus saving time and money previously required for expensive facilities and experiments
16. Air-breathing propulsion	Lightweight, fuel-efficient engines using atmospheric oxygen to support combustion
17. High-power microwaves	Microwave radiation at high power levels for weapon applications to disable sensors temporarily or permanently, or to do structural damage.
18. Pulsed power	Generation of power in the field with relatively lightweight, low-volume devices
19. Hypervelocity projectiles	Generation and use of hypervelocity projectiles to (1) penetrate hardened targets, and (2) increase the weapon's effective range
20. High-temperature, high-strength, lightweight composite materials	Materials possessing high strength, low weight, and/or able to withstand high temperatures for aerospace and other applications
21. Superconductivity	Fabrication and exploitation of superconducting materials
22. Biotechnology materials and processing	Systematic application of biology for an end use in military engineering or medicine

Source: Julian Moxon, "U.S. Technology on the Critical List," *Flight International* (June 17, 1989): 59–62.

ADVANCED AUTOMATION (part of Development and Logistics): plans for the introduction of new automated capability into the national airspace system

The FAA is not strictly autonomous. There are governmental bodies and nongovernmental organizations that exert pressure, power, and influence over the FAA's regulatory prerogatives. For example, in addition to being a part of the Department of Transportation under the cabinet secretary of transportation, the FAA is subject to political pressures from the following congressional agencies (*WID,* 589).

GENERAL ACCOUNTING OFFICE: evaluates FAA performance and issues public critiques

HOUSE AND SENATE APPROPRIATIONS COMMITTEES: appropriates FAA funding

HOUSE PUBLIC WORKS AND TRANSPORTATION COMMITTEE (Subcommittee on Aviation): legislative jurisdiction over airport funding, airline deregulation, safety issues, and FAA

HOUSE SCIENCE, SPACE, AND TECHNOLOGY COMMITTEE (Subcommittee on Transportation, Aviation, and Materials): legislative jurisdiction over civil aviation research and development

SENATE COMMERCE, SCIENCE, AND TRANSPORTATION COMMITTEE (Subcommittee on Aviation): legislative jurisdiction over aeronautical research and development and safety issues

There are also several nongovernmental bodies that exert influence on the FAA (*WID,* 589).

AEROSPACE INDUSTRIES ASSOCIATION OF AMERICA: aerospace equipment manufacturers

AIR LINE PILOTS ASSOCIATION, INTERNATIONAL (ALPA): association of airline pilots

AIR TRANSPORT ASSOCIATION (ATA) OF AMERICA: U.S. scheduled air carriers

AIRCRAFT OWNERS AND PILOTS ASSOCIATION (AOPA): general aviation aircraft owners and pilots

GENERAL AVIATION MANUFACTURERS ASSOCIATION (GAMA): general aviation aircraft and supplies manufacturers

NATIONAL AIR CARRIER ASSOCIATION: charter and scheduled air carriers

NATIONAL BUSINESS AIRCRAFT ASSOCIATION (NBAA): companies that operate corporate aircraft

REGIONAL AIRLINE ASSOCIATION: regional airlines

Other influential groups make a major contribution to establishing standards for avionics equipment. The following organizations make recommendations to the FAA on the technical design aspects of avionics.

RADIO TECHNICAL COMMISSION FOR AERONAUTICS (RTCA) (*WID*, 591): consists of members from federal agencies, aviation organizations, and industry; develops minimum operational performance standards (MOPS) for specific equipment; committees include, for example, SC-165 Satcom, SC-171 Microwave Landing System, SC-147 TCAS Airborne Equipment, SC-142 Mode S Airborne Equipment, SC-159 Minimum Aviation System Performance Standards for GPS, etc.

SOCIETY OF AUTOMOTIVE ENGINEERS (SAE): convenes committees to prepare recommendations for equipment operational standards; for example, G-10 Aerospace Behavioral Engineering Technology Committee, A-4 Aircraft Instruments Committee, S-7 Handling Qualities of Transport Category Aircraft Committee

AERONAUTICAL RADIO, INC. (ARINC): establishes recommended avionics standards, such as for the ARINC 429 and ARINC 629 buses

Major users such as individual airline manufacturers and operators can have a significant voice on the standardization committees of RTCA, SAE, and ARINC. User groups represent the interests of their members at both the bottom level, where recommendations are tendered, and at the top level (congressional and regulatory agencies), where standards are established and enforced.

Apparent aberrations can occur in jurisdictional authority, such as the U.S. Coast Guard's responsibility for the network of LORAN-C transmitting chains used, in part, for area navigation, mostly by general aviation aircraft. Until the 1980s, LORAN-C was used almost exclusively by maritime operators as a long-range oceanic navigation system. In the early 1980s, however, some innovative avionics manufacturers developed LORAN-C receivers with extensive databases of airport and waypoint locations so that aircraft could navigate with respect to these stored database fixes. Inexpensive LORAN-C avionics units were developed, and an explosion of LORAN-C use occurred for aviation. Nevertheless, the control of LORAN-C is retained by the Coast Guard, which, like the FAA, is a separate agency within the Department of Transportation.

At the international level the principal organization that works for international standards is ICAO, the International Civil Aviation Organization. ICAO was formally organized on April 4, 1947, for the purpose of encouraging and developing air navigation facilities for international civil aviation. ICAO produces International Standards documents relating to safety or regularity of international air navigation. It also produces Recommended Practices documents related to desirable practices in the interest of safety, regularity, or efficiency of international air navigation. Also, it carries out studies on technical subjects and distributes ICAO circulars to contracting states. ICAO is a very influential body and is accepted as the predominant organization for establishing international avionics standards in the interest of facilitating worldwide air transportation.

The domestic political thicket and international diplomacy are complex interrelated constraints on the FAA's regulatory authority. Worldwide avionics standardization is necessary and will be even more so as the world continues to shrink with increasing air travel. Dealing with the political influences is a continuing challenge for the FAA. Domestic and international coordination is exceedingly complex, but it must be considered as part of the framework within which avionics evolves.

The political effects on future avionics can be direct and significant, and there are several examples that can be cited. The political maneuverings related to the development of collision-avoidance systems have been very interesting. Public opinion played a large role in forcing Congress to push the FAA to have the current versions of TCAS (traffic-alert and collision-avoidance system) implemented. This whole situation dates back to 1956, when two airliners collided high over the Grand Canyon. Public outcry at that time brought Congress and the avionics industry to attention, and, with airline funding, the search for effective collision-avoidance techniques began. It was foiled by technology limitations at the time, but efforts continued at a low level with peaks at each midair occurrence. Meanwhile, the FAA wanted to pull the air traffic control system more tightly into the collision-avoidance picture. So in 1975, the idea of using transponders to communicate altitude while closure situations are computed by the aircraft TCAS system gave new impetus to the development of collision-avoidance equipment.

It was not until August 1986 that the Cerritos, California, midair collision involving an Aeromexico airliner and a Piper PA-28 stimulated Congress to put renewed pressure on the FAA to bring the current TCAS development to a production stage. The FAA has since imposed regulations to require TCAS installation in airliners. Also stimulating Congress at the time was a doubling of near-miss reports since 1983. Looking back, we see that political influence has played a large role in the evolution of collision-avoidance avionics over the last thirty years.

Collision-avoidance equipment, born out of public outcry and subsequent congressional reaction, continued as a political hot potato even as TCAS systems were being deployed. Consider the following emotional reaction (Tippins 1988a, 12): "It is wrong of the Congress (in ignorance and political panic) and duplicitous of the FAA (which we can presume knows better) to require the airlines to spend millions of dollars on TCAS while allowing other airplanes to operate in controlled airspace without altitude monitoring (Mode C), thus compromising the safety of hundreds of thousands of passengers, private and commercial, every day." Due to this kind of political pressure, the FAA now requires the use of Mode C transponders in all terminal control areas. Additionally, a Mode C requirement for aircraft operating within a thirty-nautical-mile radius of a terminal control area took effect July 1, 1989.

During the deployment stage of TCAS, the Air Transport Association (ATA) supported the FAA's requirement for installation of TCAS 2 on airliners, while the Air Line Pilots Association (ALPA) preferred TCAS 3. Through lobbying, ALPA has influenced Congress to fund further development of TCAS 3.

Mode S transponders are used in conjunction with TCAS equipment to transmit and respond to TCAS interrogations for the purpose of detecting possible aircraft conflict. Therefore, the political influence on TCAS will have the same effect for Mode S transponders. These transponders also have a datalink capability for the purpose of digital transmission of AERA clearances and other information such as weather data. In this regard, Mode S datalink capability will likely be affected by the same political influences that affect the AERA program, particularly Stage 3 of AERA (see section 2.2). That is, if and when AERA 3 gets a big push, the Mode S datalink capability will likewise be emphasized.

Windshear detection is another area in which public pressure has forced development of avionics capability. Public pressure caused Congress to pressure the FAA into forcing the airlines to install windshear-detection equipment.

The microwave landing system (MLS) involves political influence also. The MLS concept was first proposed by ICAO in 1972, when it became evident that the instrument landing system (ILS) system had some deficiencies. For many years, the FAA has billed MLS as the replacement for ILS on the basis that MLS is not so affected by electromagnetic disturbances and that MLS approach paths can be defined to be curved or segmented to facilitate concurrent approaches from many directions and approaches over unusual terrain. Users have tended to resist the introduction of MLS on the basis of cost and because ILS has been improved and is no longer as objectionable as it once was. Congress has been caught in the middle between the FAA and the user groups. In a sense, Congress is like a judge who must rule for or against MLS to break the logjam. It is a matter of economics for users, who would prefer not to incur the cost of the MLS switchover if it is not absolutely necessary. For the FAA and Congress it is a matter of planning for future arrival densities, when MLS can significantly outdo ILS. It is always difficult to make political decisions on the basis of providing future capability when it has such far-reaching economic impact.

The phasing-in of the global positioning system (GPS) as a navigation source also has political aspects, but GPS is not as controversial as MLS. GPS is currently classed by the FAA as navigation capability that is not sole-means. That is, GPS can be used for navigation in conjunction with other approved nav sources, but it cannot be used alone. Because GPS is such a sweeping change in navigation, it will phase in over a period of many years. Meanwhile, as it comes into use, the FAA and users alike can evaluate its accuracy and reliability. No doubt as time goes on, as integrity, reliability, and confidence increase, at some point GPS will be approved as a sole means of navigation. At the international level there is still skepticism about embracing GPS because of U.S. military control over the system's operation and accuracy. Meanwhile, subtle political influence may increase the use of GPS so that other nav means, such as VOR, VLF/Omega, LORAN-C, etc., can be phased out. This influence will certainly result in widespread military use of GPS, but extensive civil use could even precede military use.

Another example of potential political influence in the world of avionics is the emerging satellite communications area. The Inmarsat forty-government consortium is establishing satellite communication capability for aircraft purposes. Since the consortium is government funded, the political influence extends to diplomatic levels to ensure international access, compatibility standards, usage fees, etc. Satellite communication, commonly called satcom, is discussed in more detail in section 7.4.

On another satellite front, the members of the Future Air Navigation Systems (FANS) committee of ICAO made a diplomatic decision to avoid showing favor for any particular satellite navigation system. They learned from experience in the 1940s and 1950s that any such specific recommendations of short-range navigation aids can create tensions in the worldwide community of avionics developers and users. Instead, the FANS committee is generating a required navigation performance capability (RNPC) specification against which any particular future satnav system can be evaluated.

It is clear that political influence can play a major role in future avionics capability, since future avionics must be compatible with the airspace navigation and communication systems available and these systems are largely the result of political decisions. In an even broader sense in the global world, nav and com systems are established as international standards, and therefore, politics can play a significant role in establishing these standards.

Politics, or more specifically, governmental action, can play a more direct role in the evolution of onboard avionics by affecting the technological trends that are the basis of equipment advances. The government funds space and military programs that it believes will result in technological breakthroughs adaptable for future avionics use. One significant example is the VHSIC (very high speed integrated circuit) technology program, which has had major success in reducing the size of integrated circuitry. Robert Castellano (1986, 119) summarized its significance: "The VHSIC program was initially seen as a means of pushing commercial efforts faster than the private sector was capable of doing without DoD support. The DoD historically has stimulated growth in the private sector by giving commercial companies initial experience in manufacturing high-priced military devices. . . . Knowledge gained from DoD-funded projects helped stimulate innovative semiconductor device design and manufacture." Tobias Naegele (1989, 101) concurred: "The legacy for VHSIC is that by setting clear technical goals, we got companies to push forward much faster than they would have otherwise. Some contractors say they're three to five years ahead of where they would have been without the program." With VHSIC technology, more electronic capability can be compressed into integrated circuits. The result is that more and more electronic functional capability is squeezed into smaller and smaller packages, thereby resulting in higher speed, smaller size, lower power consumption, and more functional capability.

The military arena tends to be the leader in developing futuristic display capability, such as digital maps. Digital map generation involves high-powered graphics capability for displaying terrain and feature representations for low-flying military missions. When this kind of capability is developed to the point of being cost-effective for commercial avionics use, avionics units will be developed for displaying airport-vicinity terrain and obstacle symbology for all-weather use. This will result in more accurate and safe instrument-approach capability for all aircraft so equipped.

Through political influence, governmental action can also establish standards, such as protocols for bus and datalink transmissions and data storage standards for new high-capacity storage media, like optical disks or magnetic "smart" cards. Establishing common standards facilitates the development of systems, including avionics, around these standards. With higher levels of integration, common standards are important for compatibility during the integration process. Without common standards, additional interfacing schemes are necessary, resulting in higher cost, weight, power, etc.

According to Julian Moxon (1989, 59), "an important, but often controversial method for stimulating fundamental research in industry is the Independent Research and Development (IRAD) system, in which the Government pays for part of an internally generated R&D programme related to a Government contract." IRAD contracts serve to focus industrial research programs into areas that show promise for improving technical capability when industry may otherwise feel the business payback is lacking.

U.S. technological leadership in the past has been dependent to a significant extent on government stimulation. This government involvement in the early 1990s is in danger of being reduced to an insignificant level because of the national budget deficit that will tighten the government's purse strings. Moxon (1989, 60) expresses a common concern: "If the DoD is unwilling to sink money into far-sighted projects that might be of benefit to itself, and if NASA continues to be underfunded, how is the USA supposed to maintain its prestigious technological leadership?" Political influences, then, can have significant impact on the development of future avionics. This impact is on multiple levels. One level is the development timeframe, as indicated in the case of TCAS. Another level is the introduction level, as in the cases of MLS and AERA. Still another level is the technology support level, as in the case of VHSIC technology. When forecasting future avionics, one must consider such political influence carefully. This influence can be very fickle, though, since it depends to a degree on public mood and national economic viability. In times of national prosperity, for example, the public and Congress are more willing to support technological advancement. Therefore, forecasters of avionics trends must also forecast national and international conditions that affect the political process.

2.5. Business Concerns

Like many high-tech industries, the avionics business involves state-of-the-art technology, and this, in itself, invokes a dichotomy. On the one hand, a leader in some form of advanced technology has a leg up on the competition and therefore can establish a product leadership position. On the other hand, with technology advancing as rapidly as it does, it sometimes behooves developers to let others incur the risks of developing the market for a particular technology, and then enter the same market using more-advanced technology. Although, as Andrew Messina (1989, 50) says, "technology is recognized as potentially the single most important source of competitive advantage," product cost cannot be downgraded from its vital importance. It generally takes a great deal of capital and time to develop a product. It can pay a developer to enter the market late with a superior product based on the lessons learned by the competition.

In the world of high-tech avionics, the foothold a company establishes by developing a new product can be short-lived, simply because by the time a product goes from the concept stage through the development stage to the production stage, its technology may be somewhat less than state of the art. The competition, however, can bypass the concept stage, begin at the development stage, and produce a similar product that is higher in quality and capability in a shorter time.

It can be difficult in any kind of business, but especially in the avionics business, to introduce a new kind of product because of the market, political, and regulatory constraints. That is not to say that new product types are impossible to introduce. However, the avionics development business has several built-in constraints. New equipment must have

Regulatory approval (in the United States, FAA certification)
User acceptance by pilots and crewmembers (be useful and easy to operate)
Compatibility with existing types of ground- and space-based nav and com facilities
Cost-effectiveness in terms of acquisition and life-cycle cost

There are, therefore, significant constraints on being innovative with new operational capability. Communication frequencies and modulation modes, for example, are standardized, navigation system types are established, flight control modes are limited in number, etc. However, innovation does still occur (e.g., satcom, satnav, Doppler weather radar, fly-by-wire and sidestick controllers, electronic library system). When functional creativity in avionics does surface, it must still be compatible with the established framework of the national airspace system and must be evaluated and accepted at the international level.

Even though innovation in operational capability is limited, there is ample room for innovation in the form of technology implementation for avionics. There is a continuing push to make avionics smaller, lighter, cooler, more reliable, etc. New technical advances will continue to be folded in to avionics equipment to achieve these goals.

In section 2.4, I mentioned the political aspects of satellite communication. There are also business aspects, such as the competition that the airline-owned AvSat company was giving to the international government-controlled consortium called Inmarsat. By governmental agreement, Inmarsat had to provide global access and service, while the privately owned AvSat had no such requirement. AvSat wanted to pursue its business interest by providing service where the demand, and therefore the financial returns, was the greatest, but the FCC denied the necessary access (see section 7.4). Private businesses like AvSat, however, can pursue revenue-producing ventures such as passenger telephone service instead of ATC communication.

The future of satcom will depend to a large extent on satellite capacity (that is, the number of communication channels) because it is this capacity that will determine user cost. The projections are that capacity will increase significantly, thereby reducing the per-channel costs and making satcom more affordable to more users. As this happens, the satcom business will be self-boosting, which is an important aspect of business success.

Like most companies, avionics companies usually prefer to produce standard off-the-shelf products rather than customized products. The development costs of new or modified equipment need to be amortized over as many produced units as possible to lessen the development cost impact and to keep the product competitive.

Avionics companies periodically do a market analysis as part of their strategic planning process. When users express a need or desire for new functional capability, or if a developer can offer new functions that would be well received in the market, then further analysis is done to determine feasibility with regard to compatibility issues and cost-effectiveness before development begins.

Most new avionics equipment emerges as a result of a customer-expressed desire or need. It is also possible, but more difficult, to introduce a new product without having an acknowledged desire or need. To be successful, this kind of new product, once introduced, must of its own accord generate its market by virtue of the product's desirable attributes. An example of this was the introduction of aircraft LORAN-C receivers in the early 1980s. LORAN-C had been used for many years before its debut in the avionics arena, but it took an entrepreneurial move on the part of some avionics developers to add processing capability and a large database of airport and waypoint locations to introduce LORAN-C to avionics buyers. The introduction was a sweeping success because the product sold itself in terms of its tremendous usefulness, and it created its own instant market. Flat-panel displays may follow a similar course, but for now flat-panel technology seems to be manufacturer-driven.

With increasing levels of avionics bus integration, an important business consideration is that new equipment be compatible with existing systems. The first line of compatibility is the electrical interface between the new equipment and the host system. If direct compatibility does not exist, then separate interfacing is necessary, which is an undesirable situation. It requires more space, power, wires, connections, weight, etc. Therefore, avionics developers strive to design system compatibility into equipment. The open systems interconnection (OSI) scheme has been devised for compatibility and interoperability to reduce costs and the other factors already mentioned. This also eases line-replaceable unit (LRU) interchange and increases competition, ultimately resulting in higher quality, more reliability, improved performance, etc.

As the trend toward avionics functional integration increases (see section 4.1), airplane customers will have fewer choices for equipment and subsystems, since the integrated system will probably receive FAA certification as an entity, at least initially. Any changes would require expensive recertification. This phenomenon of "winner takes all" in the avionics business has the detrimental effect of decreasing competition with the potential ramifications of increasing costs and stifling innovation.

In the long term, integrated modular avionics systems will mature and prove their functional integrity at the module level. This will stimulate competition to offer both software and hardware modules.

From a business perspective, one other trend seems clear. Airframe companies and airlines alike appear to be expecting avionics suppliers to share more of the development risks than ever before. This expectation should result in closer teaming arrangements and strategic business partnerships between customers (airframe companies and airlines) and suppliers (avionics vendors).

Even on the military side, business factors seem to be playing a more important role in aircraft programs than ever before. As Bill Sweetman (1991, 57) reports about the air force advanced tactical fighter (ATF) contest (see section 3.2), "The winning aircraft was not selected on the basis of its flight performance, but because the US Air Force (USAF) felt that its builders were better prepared to deliver their aircraft on time and within budget. There is reason to believe the YF-23 was superior to the YF-22 in the qualities which the USAF originally stressed." Sweetman continues, "In the areas formally evaluated by the USAF—technical performance, programme structure and cost—the main differences between Lockheed's 21,000-page proposal and Northrop's proposal seem to have been in programme management and past contract performance." However, air force secretary Donald B. Rice, who announced the winning decision (*Air Force Magazine* 1991, 13), said that "the YF-22 was judged to offer better capability at a lower cost." In any case, each of the two ATF contenders vied to win the ATF full-scale development contract by investing about $170 million of company money.

Another interesting program to follow is the FSX aircraft program (see section 3.2). This aircraft is being jointly developed and produced by the United States and Japan. From a business standpoint, Japan hopes to secure key aircraft technologies and engineering capabilities, while the United States hopes to gain knowledge of Japan's production processes.

2.6. Summary

Avionics trends must be considered within the framework that provides both stimulation and constraints for evolution. Many factors must be considered as part of this framework, including the users, the environment within which avionics operate (such as the air traffic control system), the technology available, governmental stimulation and regulation, industrial standards, and the avionics business climate.

Avionics must be compatible with the ground- and space-based communication and navigation facilities that make up the national and international airspace systems. The air traffic control system is also part of the airspace system, and future avionics trends must be considered with respect to the future ATC system. Section 2.2 describes the FAA's plan for an automated enroute ATC (AERA) system that will involve a high level of ATC automation that generates clearances and communicates information to and from aircraft. Aircraft operating within the system will need to be compatible with this automated ATC system, which implies that the onboard avionics systems will need to become more automated. In the FAA's view, air traffic controllers and pilots will act as system observers and managers and will intervene in the automatic activity only when required. There is a great deal of controversy over removing the human from the control sequence, both on the ground (ATC) and in the air. This controversy will play a major role in the automation scenario. It is difficult to estimate the outcome, and predictions should be examined critically and somewhat skeptically. The student of avionics trends needs to be aware of the issues, the pros and cons, and the many factors that will affect the outcome. One thing that seems certain is that as air traffic becomes more congested, there will be tighter air traffic control required to maintain safety, and this will lead to the need for increased automation. It is unclear, though, what will happen to the human role and the level of manual operation in the cockpit.

The intent of AERA is to increase airport and enroute capacity by enhancing enroute control, expediting departure and arrival sequencing, and reducing separation standards to accommodate the future increase in air traffic densities, all while maintaining sufficient safety standards. Achieving this means direct routings, optimized altitude assignments, inflight time savings, and maximized fuel economy.

Another aspect of the framework within which avionics is evolving is the changing technology that makes avionics possible. Part of this technology is state-of-the-art intersystem busing schemes. Digital buses such as MIL-STD-1773 and ARINC 629 will become more common for standardized interfacing of LRUs. Generally, fiber-optic buses will become more common than wire buses for most purposes, and high-speed buses on the order of 50 megabits per second will be introduced. This trend facilitates higher levels of system integration in advanced data-intensive avionics systems.

Flat-panel displays will be introduced into cockpits in the 1990s. Over time, these displays will become larger and larger, making possible less cluttered and more intuitive display formats.

The decade of the 1980s saw the virtual elimination of analog technology from advanced avionics. The analog-to-digital transformation is a foregone conclusion, and the decade of the 1990s will see significant improvements in advanced avionics, made possible by continuing advances in digital technology and applications. With projections of 100-million-gate ICs by the year 2000, the resulting functional performance in avionics almost defies today's comprehension.

The government's VHSIC program stimulated device-level advances from which avionics equipment will benefit. GaAs devices are providing low-noise, high-speed capability. In the future, combination RISC/CISC processors will combine the advantages of each (speed and application capability). Neural networks will be employed along with artificial intelligence in new, more powerful avionics applications, such as real-time decision aiding. While today's 80860 runs at 40 MHz, tomorrow's microprocessors will achieve 100-MHz speeds. By the year 2000, with highly dense microprocessors, "significant improvements in the area of human interfaces are probable: speech generation and recognition and video are some examples" (Gelsinger et al. 1989, 47). The results of all of these advances will be smaller, faster, more functional, more powerful, and more reliable avionics.

The much touted "software crisis" is having a slow but profound effect on the development of avionics software. Developers are recognizing the value of software engineering principles that emphasize software modularity, modifiability, understandability, reliability, and efficiency. Today's avionics development programs, which can involve 90 percent software, contribute to much better software development. New software development methods involving CASE tools are now available and are being improved to support the software design, development, and maintenance phases.

The expert-systems (ES) and artificial-intelligence (AI) approach to some avionics-related functions is largely an untapped resource. Applications, which include decision aiding, fault analysis, emergency handling, speech recognition, and collision avoidance, will begin to mature in the 1990s.

Other aspects of the framework within which future avionics will evolve are the regulatory and influential forces of the FAA, ICAO, and the many standards organizations such as ARINC and RTCA. These organizations establish standards for future avionics to ensure quality and compatibility on a worldwide basis. While the government regulates avionics capability through the DOT and the FAA, the government also can stimulate the avionics field through military, NASA, and academic research and development programs. Important avionics advances often come from these government-funded initiatives.

The basic tenets of business—developing products and markets in a highly competitive environment—also are a part of the framework within which advanced avionics will evolve. Avionics business decisions must take into account volatile state-of-the-art technology, avionics functional discriminators, strategic market positioning, and cost competitiveness.

3. Review of Advanced Avionics Programs

3.1. Avionics Programs

This chapter is by no means an exhaustive review of current programs; rather, it provides enough information to suggest the kinds of avionics advances that are likely to transfer from research and military programs to commercial aircraft in the 1990s and beyond.

3.1.1. Pave Pillar

The Pave Pillar program has been in progress for several years (the Phase 1 contract was awarded in 1984) under the auspices of the U.S. Air Force Aeronautical Systems Division (ASD) at Wright-Patterson Air Force Base, which is sharing the knowledge and some of the effort with the army and the navy. This is a long-term advanced avionics architecture program that is intimately associated with the air force's advanced tactical fighter (ATF) program. Its major goals are to:

- Partition the avionics systems into a set of standard functional modules, called common modules, for fault-tolerant redundancy, system reconfigurability, and graceful degradation
- Increase the level of avionics system integration, thereby improving information correlation, accuracy, fault tolerance, and sensor

resource sharing while at the same time reducing the need for redundant sensors

- Improve functional availability and mission effectiveness
- Use VHSIC technology devices (see section 2.3.2) for high-speed processing and bus interfacing, high reliability, and extensive device-level built-in test capability for ease and accuracy of flight-line fault isolation
- Incorporate the use of a high-speed (50 Mbps), wideband, fiber-optic, multiplex data-distribution bus
- Use extensive mass memory for data backup and banks of data storage
- Lower the cost of avionics ownership

The system integration aspect of the Pave Pillar program involves navigation, flight control, target acquisition and sensor-data fusion (data correlation and consolidation), weapons management, and integrated cockpit displays. The system architecture involves distributed control to achieve efficiency in resource utilization and mission effectiveness. Despite the high level of integration, the overall system has functional and reconfigurable boundaries dividing the system into the following three areas:

Mission management. Dual-redundant mission data processing for target acquisition, navigation management, defense management, stores management, terrain following and avoidance, fire control, and crew station management, including avionics diagnostic status

Sensor management. Sensor data distribution, sensor control, and signal processing

Vehicle management. Data processing for flight purposes, control and display interfaces, flight actuators and sensors, the electrical distribution system, and engine controls. The vehicle management system is quad-redundant and unintegrated with the other two areas for safety-of-flight reasons.

The Pave Pillar system uses a modular approach to the integrated architecture, which is a major contribution to the evolution of advanced avionics. The reliability goal for each module is one hundred thousand hours. High-speed VHSIC devices perform complete processing functions. Multiple modules are used together to achieve subsystem functional capability. This modular approach also permits a cost savings in spares types. With the use of a high-speed data bus and VHSIC devices, the number of cables and connectors in a system can be reduced by as much as 35 percent.

3.1.2. Pave Sprinter

Pave Sprinter is another U.S. Air Force ASD initiative, with the goal of reorienting the second and succeeding phases of the Pave Pillar program to focus on the advanced tactical fighter (ATF) avionics suite. The method to be used to accomplish this goal is to demonstrate a Pave Pillar standard modular ICNIA (integrated communication, navigation, and identification avionics) architecture on an F-16 aircraft to permit the operational capabilities of these integrated systems to be assessed. The system architecture will consist of a suite of LRMs (line-replaceable modules), forming an ICNIA system and a modular, integrated, inertial-reference system and using VHSIC technology and a high-speed fiber-optics data bus.

Another major goal is to improve the system fault-monitoring capability so that fault detection and LRM isolation may be done quickly onboard the aircraft without the need for additional test equipment.

3.1.3. Pave Pace

Pave Pace is still another ASD program that will build on the advances of the Pave Pillar program. Pave Pillar has established the system architecture for acquiring and distributing system-wide data. Under Pave Pace, a strawman (so called because it is in the initial stages) avionics system incorporating several new technological advances will be proposed for the beginning of the twenty-first century. Some of the technologies and techniques to be explored and validated by the Pave Pace program are:

AI (artificial intelligence) algorithms to assist in mission decision making

Neural-network parallel-processing capability for adaptive learning systems

Opto-electronics

Advanced packaging and flow-through cooling concepts

CAD (computer-aided design) and CAM (computer-aided manufacturing) tools

Large full-color displays with high-speed graphics processing for real-time panoramic scenes

Advanced signal-processing techniques for wideband RF (radio frequency) accumulation

Extraordinarily high speed processing using parallel-processing techniques

Pervasive use of BIT (built-in test) capability and fault-tolerant architectures

Pave Pace will culminate in integrated testbed demonstrations to show that avionics availability, performance, and cost can be significantly improved to achieve better situation awareness for the flight crew and better fault tolerance and maintainability for the system. Generally, the goals include better avionics functionality, reliability, availability, and maintainability through the use of advanced technology and techniques.

3.1.4. ICNIA (Integrated Communication, Navigation, and Identification Avionics)

The U.S. Air Force originally funded a study in 1978 to explore the feasibility of integrating CNI (com, nav, and identification) functions. Integrating these functions was desirable because the proliferation of numerous cockpit controls, instruments, switch panels, etc., was causing space and weight problems. In addition, equipment failures caused system availability and life-cycle cost problems, and the lack of equipment standardization was creating a severe logistics problem. In 1983 both the U.S. Air Force Laboratory at Wright Patterson AFB and the U.S. Army Avionics Research and Development Activity (AVRADA) at Ft. Monmouth, New Jersey, were awarded an advanced development contract for ICNIA.

The ICNIA concept is to standardize LRMs into a minimum number of common module types that serve as shared, reconfigurable resources. These module types include a radio-frequency group, a signal-processing group, and a data-processing group. Various module types, under software control, are then configured in real time to perform various com, nav, and identification functions as a given function becomes necessary. Additionally, critical modules would have one or two redundant backups, so that in the event of a module failure, the executive controller could automatically cut out the failed module and cut in a good module. The flight crew would not be aware of any functional loss. The following functions, and potentially others, are candidates for inclusion in the ICNIA system:

HF com
VHF-AM/FM com
SINCGARS (single-channel ground and airborne radio system)
Have Quick (air-ground-air jam-resistant UHF)
UHF-AM com
Seek Talk (jam-resistant voice com)
Air force satcom
JTIDS (joint tactical information-distribution system)

TACAN (tactical air navigation)
VOR/ILS (VHF omnirange/instrument landing system)
IFF (identification friend-or-foe) and Mode S transponder
GPS (global positioning system)
EPLRS (enhanced position location and reporting system)
DABS (discrete-address beacon system — Mode S transponder)
TCAS (traffic-alert and collision-avoidance system)

Benefits of the standard module concept include:

Reduced development time, parts count, and cost
Improved functional availability through reconfiguration
Simplified support logistics (reduced quantities and types of inventoriable items, easier documentation, reduced need for test equipment)
Reduced life-cycle cost

Because of dynamic and automatic system reconfigurability, for the first time ICNIA allows a deferred maintenance policy for avionics. This level of system fault tolerance permits graceful functional degradation. In addition to supporting flight-line maintenance, enhanced built-in test capability at the module level provides better fault-detection and fault-isolation capability. This decreases aircraft turnaround time and improves system availability.

The common modules are called high-density standard modules (HDSM) and measure 5.875 inches by 6.382 inches by 0.5 inches with 304-pin edge connectors. Surface-mount technology (SMT) devices are used for increased circuit density. ICNIA processor volume is reduced by a factor of six and weight is reduced by a factor of four (Poradish 1987, 22). Generally, the projected size and weight savings for production ICNIA modules are more than 50 percent (Harris 1988, 4). VHSIC technology devices are used for maximum circuit density and built-in test capability. Ceramic circuit boards reduce thermal expansion and conduct heat away from the boards.

In summary, objectives of the ICNIA program are:

- Size and weight savings
- Increased reliability
- Improved maintainability
- Reduced life-cycle costs
- Enhanced supportability
- New technology (VHSIC/SMT) insertion

3.1.5. Pilot's Associate

The Pilot's Associate program began as military research to see if the ever-increasing complexity of tasks required to be performed by fighter pilots could be kept at tolerable workload levels by employing an avionics expert systems (ES) approach to automate some pilot functions. Instead of automating certain functions, however, the Pilot's Associate system keeps the pilot fully in the control loop by providing recommendations for action and by providing situation awareness information after first assessing all available information from the aircraft sensors and from the onboard systems and extensive database. Relevant information is then presented to the pilot on three primary displays: the center display shows the tactical situation, the left display portrays the aircraft and weapons situation, and the right display gives a "big picture" enhanced tactical view.

Sponsored by the Defense Advanced Research Projects Agency (DARPA) and the U.S. Air Force Wright Aeronautical Labs (AFWAL) in conjunction, since 1985, with Lockheed and McDonnell, the Pilot's Associate program intends to develop five ES software modules that provide critical advice to a fighter pilot. These five separate knowledge-based ES functional modules are integrated by a software executive that allocates resources and coordinates the functions. The functional modules generate, analyze, update, and prioritize information continuously.

Table 3.1. Five expert-systems software modules developed by the Pilot's Associate program

Module	Function
System status	Monitors all onboard systems
	Identifies, diagnoses, anticipates, verifies, and compensates for malfunctions
	Assists pilot with normal and emergency procedures
	Informs pilot of aircraft attitude, status, and capability
Mission planning	Suggests navigation alternatives
	Plans threat avoidance
	Performs fuel analysis and management
	Devises route modification
Tactical planning	Plans offensive and defensive actions
	Tailors tactics to threat situation
	Recommends flight-path changes, threat-avoidance maneuvers, countermeasures, and weapons use
Situation assessment	Correlates external sensor information, including friendly and enemy forces, existing and forecast weather, terrain, aircraft status, and available resources
Pilot-vehicle interface	Presents the most essential information from the various systems to the pilot

Source: James H. Brahney, "High Tech Help for the Combat Pilot," *Aerospace Engineering* (Aug. 1988): 15–18.

The cockpit environment, especially in combat, saturates the pilot with information, leading to information overload. The Pilot's Associate system analyzes the information and supports the pilot in critical areas such as navigation, weapons control, damage assessment, electronic warfare, and tactical planning. Priorities and recommendations are presented to the pilot for evaluation and action. The system does not usurp the pilot's authority but manages information to permit the pilot to focus attention on priority tasks. The system automates only menial tasks that would otherwise distract the pilot. Brahney (1988, 18) describes the advantages: "During periods of low workload, the pilot normally has time to digest detailed explanations of recommended actions. However, when response time is critical, the module will recognize that fact and will deliver only essential information." Only in an extreme situation, such as pilot incapacitation, does the system take over full control. A limited demonstration program (Pohlmann and Payne 1988) proved the feasibility and potential of employing an ES approach to avionics information and flight situation management.

The Pilot's Associate program is a military project, but the same kind of artificial intelligence decision making can be applied in civilian cockpits to help alleviate pilot-error problems such as fuel mismanagement, improper flight control, and improper system operation. This becomes especially useful as the three-pilot airline flight deck is reduced to two pilots and the two-pilot corporate cockpit is reduced to one pilot.

3.1.6. Supercockpit

The principal element of the U.S. Air Force's Supercockpit program is a pilot helmet with a built-in, three-dimensional (3D), spherical visual-display system that displays tactical and flight-situation information to facilitate spatial awareness for the pilot. The ultimate goal is to permit the pilot of a sophisticated aircraft to make better use of the systems and information available while minimizing sensory overload. This program was initiated in 1986 by the Armstrong Aerospace Medical Research Lab at Wright Patterson AFB and is planned to last until the end of the century.

The many pieces of information available from the avionics, weapons, and sensor subsystems are fused, organized, and presented as a 120-degree panoramic view with auditory cues indicating the relative positions of external threats. The pilot can direct weapons fire and can issue aircraft commands using visual line-of-sight fixations and voice. The program is segregated into three phases with separate capability implemented in each phase:

Phase 1. Head-aimed fire control and night-vision infrared head-up display; ground and flight testing began in 1990

Phase 2. Down-looking "God's eye" view; perspective apparent from 20,000 feet; head, eye, and voice control of system; testing in 1993

Phase 3. Tactile control and feedback; Pilot's Associate integration; begins in 1996

This schedule does not support Supercockpit's inclusion in the U.S. Air Force's ATF program (described in section 3.2). However, the Supercockpit helmet is planned to be first used, probably with minimal capability, in fighter aircraft in the mid-1990s. It will probably be after the turn of the century before any significant Supercockpit capability will be in use. The display and visual technology is also currently being advanced as part of the U.S. Army's RAH helicopter program (see section 3.2).

With its advanced display system, the helmet is expected to weigh under three pounds when fully refined. It contains two miniature binocular CRTs with a small screen that permits a virtual 3D projection of external terrain, ground-reference symbology, other aircraft, and systems information. In the deployed version the screen will be translucent to permit actual outside see-through. The helmet's sensor system detects the direction and orientation of the pilot's head, and the scene is projected accordingly, with the image and overlying text and symbols stabilized.

Infrared imaging will be used to give the pilot good night vision. Radar data will be computer processed so that symbology may be used to represent other aircraft. Symbology will also depict nav waypoints. The idea of "virtual" switches is being developed, which involves the projection of switch images on a panel within the pilot's view. When the pilot reaches to "touch" the imaginary switch, a magnetic position-sensing device at the fingertip of the pilot's glove determines proximity of the fingertip to the switch and causes switch actuation. Likewise, a pressure device at the fingertip causes the sensation of tactile feedback upon switch activation. Speech recognition will also be used for commanding some functions, which can be a great help in combat, especially during high-G-force maneuvering. Zoom capability will permit the pilot to enlarge images for clarity. According to Thomas Furness (quoted in Lerner 1986, 22), director of the Supercockpit project, by around 1995 "the pilot will have practically no contact with real controls. He will activate everything by eye, voice, or virtual buttons."

In Phase 3, Pilot's Associate capability (see section 3.1.5) will be integrated into the Supercockpit helmet. The pilot's brain waves will be monitored to detect information overload and to permit automatic system takeover in the event that the pilot becomes incapacitated. This is the beginning of a new thrust to inform the system of pilot status in addition to the conventional method of informing the pilot of system status.

A significant level of human factors research is being done as part of the Supercockpit project to gain greater knowledge about how people relate to machines. The use of aural cues, voice commands, visual symbology, virtual switches, and panoramic, 3D scenic displays is a change of immense magnitude from today's cockpit. AI/ES will be employed to an advanced degree so that the system can provide the pilot with verbal situation analysis and advice. Technology advances in processing throughput, sensing capability, and display techniques will be achieved.

The concept of a cockpit-in-a-helmet has many major advantages.

Cockpit hardware and its associated volume, weight, power consumption, and life-cycle costs are reduced.

A pilot can use the helmet in a mission simulation mode to practice an upcoming mission.

The helmet can be used for general systems and flight-training purposes without involving the aircraft.

To an extent, cockpit standardization can be achieved.

In a battle situation, the actual cockpit can be completely encapsulated to protect the pilot from radiation flashes and other combat hazards.

The virtual cockpit can be adapted for changing requirements without involving cockpit hardware changes.

Some particularly hazardous missions can be flown remotely, with the pilot safely on the ground but still fully in control of the mission.

While the Supercockpit concept is being developed for high-performance fighters, benefits of the technological breakthroughs will eventually spill over to commercial use.

3.2. Aircraft Programs

Several advanced aircraft programs involve advanced avionics. New aircraft development programs offer the best potential for including new avionics capability and new technology. The observer of avionics trends is encouraged to keep tabs on new aircraft programs for this reason.

Naturally, of course, even new aircraft programs must temper the desire to incorporate the best and the latest with the cost-constraint requirement. Nevertheless, it is the new aircraft programs that tend to indicate the direction of current trends in avionics. This section provides a brief summary of these programs and some of the associated avionics-related activity in order to permit the reader to follow the avionics developments associated with the aircraft.

ATF (Advanced Tactical Fighter). The U.S. Air Force's advanced tactical fighter, designated the F-22, is a next-generation high-technology replacement for the F-15, which dates back to 1974. The ATF program originated in 1981 and was boosted with a $64 billion dollar contract award to Lockheed, General Dynamics, and Boeing on April 23, 1991. Flight testing is expected to begin in 1995, and the U.S. Air Force expects to acquire more than six hundred ATFs by the end of deliveries in 2014. Production should begin in 1997, with the first operational squadron expected around 2002. At full production, forty-eight aircraft per year will be delivered.

Because the aircraft production run is expected to be high and avionics will make up to half the cost of next-generation fighters, there is a great effort by the contractors to develop high-performance avionics with high reliability and high maintainability. As John Rhea stated (1986, 1211), "ATF is probably the single most important program for the electronics industry in terms of both dollars and technological advances." The avionics will be very highly integrated and based on the Pave Pillar modular architecture (see section 3.1.1). It is estimated that there will be at least 320 liquid-cooled modules, of which thirty-three will be unique. Most of the modules will use Intel's 80960 32-bit RISC processor architectures. The redundant common-module approach provides high fault-tolerant system reliability with reconfigurability and graceful degradation. Within the modules, VHSIC devices (see section 2.3.2) will be used extensively for high throughput performance. In addition, the VHSIC devices have extensive built-in test capability for device-level fault detection in support of the high fault isolation and maintainability requirements of the ATF program.

The Pave Pillar architecture incorporates Joint Integrated Avionics Working Group (JIAWG) standards. It is integrated with a 50-Mbps multiplex fiber-optic data bus and may also use dedicated high-bandwidth buses in the range of 100 to 200 Mbps. The fiber-optics bus has the advantages of immunity from electromagnetic interference, electronic countermeasures, and electromagnetic pulse effects. A parallel interface (PI) bus and test/maintenance (TM) bus will also be used. The following areas highlight the ATF's avionics:

Emphasis on passive FLIR (forward-looking infrared) and millimeter-wave radiometric sensors with high resolution; IRST (infrared search and track) capability will be employed in later models to track infrared signatures of targets; sensors will acquire, track, and engage targets beyond visual range before the ATF is detectable; radar antennas will be active-element (3,000 elements) phased-array stealth versions

MIMIC (microwave/millimeter-wave monolithic integrated circuits) sensors using GaAs solid-state devices as an alternative to traveling wave tubes and klystrons for high reliability radar

VHSIC (very high speed integrated circuits) for common signal processors

ICNIA (integrated com, nav, and IFF avionics) distributed architecture includes VHF and UHF com modules as well as TACAN, GPS, and MLS/ILS modules; IFF transponder; JTIDS (joint tactical information-distribution system); RF tactical datalink

INEWS (integrated electronic warfare system) modular electronic warfare avionics with capability of automatic target detection and classification

Fly-by-wire flight control

Digital electronic engine controls

Low-observable antennas

Aspects of Pilot's Associate capability (see section 3.1.5), providing AI and ES decision aiding

Seven high-resolution color LCD flat-panel displays (one 8-by-8-inch, two 6-by-6-inch, two 4-by-4-inch, and two smaller units); possibly 3D-holographic HUD

Software-based functionality using ADA, which has multitasking capability

Supercockpit capability (see section 3.1.6) will be included to the extent that it is mature; provides "big picture" situation awareness, reduces pilot workload by managing subsystems and information, and permits the pilot to cope with and respond to priorities during high-stress or threat situations.

The technology that is actually deployed will depend on the maturity of each item at the time of the go/no-go decisions. For example, speech recognition and synthesis as well as fly-by-light fiber optics are doubtful. A helmet-mounted display will probably be added as an option later. The benefits of the ATF's advanced avionics are obvious: reduced pilot workload, better system capability, increased reliability and maintainability, and lower cost.

ATA (Advanced Tactical Aircraft). The U.S. Navy's A-12 advanced tactical aircraft was intended, before its cancellation in January 1991, as the replacement for the Grumman A-6 Intruder before the year 2000. The prime contractors included General Dynamics and McDonnell Douglas. Well before the cancellation, the General Accounting Office estimated that $7 billion could be saved by adapting the ATF for naval use rather than developing a totally different aircraft (Dudney 1989, 52). However, the navy wanted to use the airplane as a subsonic long-range attack fighter. In contrast, the air force ATF is intended to be a supersonic air-superiority (highly maneuverable) fighter.

The navy had an office at Wright-Patterson to work with the air force in developing preliminary system specs for the navy version of the ATF, referred to as the NATF. The NATF could have had approximately 60 percent commonality with the ATF, mostly in the area of systems. However, the airframe structures of the NATF need to be stronger than those of the ATF to withstand carrier landings, so the navy will probably continue to fly F-14s until about 1997. A new joint navy–air force initiative could result in a next-generation interdiction fighter called the AX, which might become the NATF or a derivative of the original A-12. Tentative planning suggests that the AX could be operational by 2012.

The navy's avionics advances will probably include the transition from analog to digital equipment, VHSIC and MIMIC component technology, high-speed optical databuses integrating a fail-soft distributed system architecture, a fly-by-wire (possibly fly-by-light) flight control system, new improved radar, advanced sensors (such as passive infrared sensors), sensor fusion to integrate sensor data, electronic support measures, and other military-specific kinds of avionics.

The canceled A-12 had 8-by-8-inch color LCD flat-panel displays. Bruce D. Nordwall (1989, 56) notes their significance: "This is the first known use of liquid crystal displays (LCDs) of this size for a major military aircraft program." The state-of-the-art avionics for the A-12 accounted for up to 40 percent of the aircraft's cost.

ATB (B-2 Advanced Technology Bomber). While the ATF's emphasis is on significant performance improvements over the F-15, the ATB's emphasis is not on performance at all but on low-observability technologies for a reduced radar cross-section to avoid radar detection. The advanced technology of the U.S. Air Force's ATB depends more on its airframe shape and materials than on its systems. The ATB's weight, speed, and payload are estimated to be less than those of the B-1B, but its radar cross-section is estimated at half that of the B-1B. The stealth technology being used to achieve radar detection avoidance includes:

> Smooth, rounded, and irregular airframe shape for radar directivity away from the radar source
> Use of radar-absorbent and deflecting materials and structures (the ATB is made mostly of composite materials)
> Thermal reduction of aircraft skin and exhaust

The ATB's systems are still largely classified, but speculation suggests (Sweetman 1989, 25) that some of the key avionics items are:

> Sophisticated fly-by-wire flight control system for automatic adjustment of the control surfaces for stability (the ATB flying wing is inherently unstable without stability augmentation), along with the use of thrust vectoring for the same purpose
> Low probability-of-intercept (LPI) reconnaissance radar
> State-of-the-art electronic support measures (ESM)
> Electro-optic sensors
> Electronic warfare (EW) systems
> Mission management systems with 3D nav capability
> Large cockpit displays

The prime contractor for the ATB is Northrop of Pico Rivera, California, which is subcontracting with Boeing Advanced Systems and LTV Aircraft Products Group for major airframe components and with General Electric's Engine Group. The prototype unveiling occurred at Northrop's Palmdale plant on November 22, 1988. Federal budget concerns and political considerations make the B-2's future uncertain.

RAH-66 Comanche (Reconnaissance Attack Helicopter). The U.S. Army's RAH-66 Comanche helicopter (originally called the LHX for light helicopter experimental) was conceived to be an advanced technology and highly integrated single-pilot combat helicopter. According to *Defence Helicopter World* (Colucci 1986, 40), "More than any helicopter before, LHX will rely on electronics and the careful integration of sophisticated systems." The military's MANPRINT (manpower and personnel integration) program is being applied to the RAH to ensure that the technology being developed is integrated with the pilot and maintenance personnel in mind.

The program has had a very turbulent history since its inception in 1983. The avionics complement involves a very ambitious array of high-tech units and, as such, has been subject to congressional scepticism and Pentagon criticism from the beginning. The year 1987 was particularly difficult for the program. Because of concern over technological maturity and single-pilot feasibility, Congress reduced funding for the program. The army was forced into accepting the two-pilot cockpit and had to downscale the admittedly ambitious program. The Pentagon also directed the army to explore the possibility of upgrading the AH-64 Apache and the UH-60 Blackhawk as alternatives to pursuing the LHX program.

The program started with a planned quantity of 4,500 helicopters and an IOC (initial operational capability) expected during 1992. After the program was restructured in 1987, the total quantity was reduced to 2,096 descoped single-purpose scout-attack helicopters. The flight of the first prototype is expected in 1994. Production of 1,292 RAH-66 Comanches is expected to run from 1995 (first delivery in 1996) to 2005, with IOC occurring by late 1998. Some of the major goals of the program include:

- Reduced pilot workload that still keeps the pilot in the loop (major human factors achievements are expected)
- Night nap-of-the-earth (NOE) flight capability at highest forward speed (approximately 190 knots)
- System integration at a very high level
- System fault tolerance, reconfigurability, graceful degradation, and better supportability through using the Pave Pillar modular architecture (see section 3.1.1)

The highly integrated avionics architecture involves redundant common modules with spares, dual system buses, and extensive built-in test capability to achieve fault tolerance.

Even before the program crisis in 1987, in an effort to prove the viability of state-of-the-art systems, an advance program called ARTI (advanced rotorcraft technology integration) was undertaken by the army. The ARTI program was a mission task and workload study of many of the technology risk areas of the proposed LHX program. These risk areas were:

Helmet-mounted displays (spin-off of the Supercockpit concept)
Electro-optic target-recognition system

Fault-tolerant architecture
Touchscreen
Speech recognition
Single-pilot feasibility

The focal point of the advanced technology integrated and automated cockpit is the Comanche's mission equipment package (MEP). It is said to account for 50 to 60 percent of the aircraft's cost and includes:

Pave Pillar modular distributed architecture for fault and battle-damage tolerance (a common approach with air force and navy)

50-MHz high-speed optical data bus

Dual triple-redundant fly-by-wire flight control system with side-stick controller

Advanced target acquisition and designation system with automatic or aided target-recognition and tracking capability; includes sensor fusion of high-sensitivity (low-light) television, FLIR, and laser rangefinder/designator

Wide-field-of-view helmet-mounted display with FLIR and image intensification sensors; includes night-vision pilotage system (NVPS), also called pilot night-vision system (PNVS)

1.25 micron VHSIC device 32-bit signal and data processors (Intel 80960)

Integrated aircraft survivability equipment (ASE): radar warning receiver, radar jamming, infrared jamming

Digital moving-terrain map display

Speech recognition and command system

Integrated core avionics architecture using VHSIC signal and data processors; ICNIA that includes GPS

Color, flat-panel, multifunction, 6-by-8-inch high-resolution displays for nav and tactical situation, with touch and voice control

Integrated electronic warfare system (INEWS); RAH will contain the army's first fully integrated EW combat system

The mission equipment package (MEP) being developed for the RAH is intended to establish a common mission package for all future army helicopters. A tri-service Joint Integrated Avionics Working Group (JIAWG) was established by the DOD to define the common avionics architecture for the RAH, the air force's ATF, and the navy's ATA in order to ensure future module compatibility.

A twenty-three-month demonstration/evaluation (dem/val) phase of the RAH program began October 31, 1988 and ended in September 1990. The purpose of the dem/val phase was to evaluate the system's design, performance, operational effectiveness, and survivability and to finalize the MEP avionics suite. Most of this proof-of-concept was accomplished by using computer simulation since no flying prototype existed during this phase.

The highest risk items for the RAH received special attention during dem/val to reduce these risks prior to full-scale development (FSD). These high-risk areas include the electro-optical sensors for target acquisition, the VHSIC-based mission computers, digital map, voice interactive control, and the helmet-mounted display system with night-vision capability. Even the redundancy level of the modules is likely to be reduced. It is possible that the ICNIA and INEWS subsystems may be eliminated, too, because of their cost and weight.

EFA (European Fighter Aircraft). The EFA program originated in the early 1980s, when Great Britain, West Germany, Italy, Spain, and France investigated the feasibility of forming a consortium to develop a modern, new-technology, stealth fighter aircraft to be marketed worldwide. Before the project really got under way, France pulled out in August 1985 to develop its own light fighter, the Dassault Rafale, which has a delivery target of 1998 and has an avionics suite comparable to the EFA. Since then, Sweden has also initiated the development of another advanced light fighter, the Saab JAS 39 Gripen. However, the fighter known as the EFA is the one being developed by the Munich-based Eurofighter company, consisting of the partners British Aerospace (BAe) of Great Britain with 33 percent ownership, Messerschmitt-Boelkow-Blohm/Dornier (MBB) of Germany with 33 percent, Aeritalia (AIT) of Italy with 21 percent, and Construcciones Aeronauticas S.A. (CASA) of Spain with 13 percent.

The EFA project is said to be Europe's most important military program and largest cooperative effort ever. The result is expected to be an initial production of at least 765 aircraft: 250 for Great Britain, 250 for Germany, 165 for Italy, and 100 for Spain. The aircraft is heavily avionics dependent and includes:

Quadruplex, digital, fly-by-wire automatic flight control system with stability augmentation and autothrottle
Digital engine controls
Wide-angle, raster-scanning, head-up display (HUD)
Three-color multifunction displays (MFDs) for flight data and systems status display

State-of-the-art nav systems, including INS, GPS, and MLS

Integrated defensive systems for detection and analysis of electromagnetic transmissions to complement the low-observable aircraft structure; automatic and manual countermeasures capability

Infrared search and track (IRST)

Direct voice input for system control

Helmet-mounted voice-warning system

Provisions for helmet-mounted sight

50-nm multimode radar for detecting, identifying, and engaging multiple targets; built-in forward-looking infrared (FLIR) system

20-MHz high-speed fiber-optics data bus

British Aerospace has the lead responsibility for the avionics systems, which are expected to be modular with forty line-replaceable units housed in six racks. BAe has also been involved with the Experimental Aircraft program (EAP) since the early 1980s. The EAP will serve as a technology demonstrator for EFA avionics, especially the systems and cockpit displays.

The EFA aims to be highly functional with modern avionics, but aircraft cost has dominated the development phase. According to Kenneth Timmerman (1987, 128), "Although technical considerations are important, the bottom line for the next generation of European fighters will be cost more than performance." As is typical for highly integrated systems, cost and weight could be half that of traditional implementations. The system specification for the EFA was frozen in September 1987. Flight testing began in 1987, and the first prototype flight is expected in 1993 with active service planned for 1997. Worldwide political and economic changes occurring in the 1990s could cause significant changes to the EFA program.

Boeing 777. This latest in the 700 series of Boeing airliners was launched in October 1990 and is planned for airline service in 1995. Its advanced avionics concepts evolved out of its predecessor, dubbed the 7J7 Advanced Technology Airliner, which was never developed. Because of the 777's dependence on the 7J7 concepts, it is worth a review of the 7J7 features first.

Boeing conceived the 7J7 project in 1984 to take advantage of advances in propulsion and avionics improvements. The propulsion system was to consist of two pusher-type unducted fan engines, each having two counter-rotating prop fans. This power system has much better propulsive efficiency and would thereby yield savings in fuel and operating costs. Also, to reduce operating costs, lightweight materials such as composites and aluminum lithium alloy were to be used in the fuselage and wing structures. Boeing engineers estimated that their propfan 7J7s would burn "an astounding 85% less fuel than the 727" (Labich 1987, 68).

Boeing proposed incorporating the following advanced avionics capabilities:

Large, color flat-panel displays to reduce volume, weight, power consumption, and cost, and to increase reliability

New high-speed bidirectional bus (ARINC 629) with electrical and optical technology for dissimilar redundancy to save wire and connector weight

Digital fly-by-wire capability for the flight control system, with flight envelope protection logic to prevent the crew from stalling or overstressing the aircraft

Onboard maintenance system (OMS) for better fault-detection and isolation capability

Flight management system (FMS) with LNAV, VNAV, and windshear-detection capability

Category 3B autoland capability

Greater use of VLSI component parts to increase performance and reduce size and weight

Inclusion of GPS and MLS for enroute and approach navigation

Emphasis on the Ada programming language with a software engineering approach

Solid-state switches and panel lighting for improved reliability and reduced weight and power

The avionics approach was to be modular with very high integration and a 30 to 50 percent reduction in the LRU count through functional consolidation. Power, weight, wires, and cooling requirements were expected to be reduced by 50 percent. Generally, the goals for the advanced avionics included improved performance, higher reliability, and reduced crew workload.

Although the program was canceled in 1987 because business factors conspired against it, much was achieved in developing advanced avionics concepts. Many of the planned concepts will reach fruition in the next-generation 777 aircraft. Like most of the latest airliners, the 777 will have a two-pilot cockpit crew. To a much higher degree than past airliners, the 777 systems will be designed with a human-factors emphasis that will maximize head-up situation awareness. The 7J7 features planned for the 777 are:

Six 8-by-8-inch color flat-panel EFIS displays, like those of the 747-400 configuration (It has been estimated that the LCD flat panels will be lighter and smaller than their CRT predecessors by a factor of one-half, the power consumption will be about half, and the MTBF reliability will be double.)

Small LCD flat panels to display speed and altitude

ARINC 629 buses provide the major connectivity between system components

Fly-by-wire flight control, introduced for the first time on Boeing airplanes (The FBW benefits include increased aerodynamic efficiency, aircraft performance envelope protection for airspeed and attitude, reduced wing and tail structural weight, and reduced maintenance costs.)

Satcom and GPS as standard funtions

Category 3B autoland capability (even with one engine failed) and provisions for Category 3C (zero ceiling, zero visibility) capability

HIRF (high-intensity radiated field) hardening and passive cooling wherever possible

Dual-redundant integrated modular cabinets with the following system functions: flight management system (FMS), onboard maintenance system (OMS) with integrated airplane condition monitoring system (ACMS) capability, and state-of-the-art datalink capability (These cabinets are designed to support extensive processing and memory growth.)

Electronic library system (ELS) provisions to serve the flight, maintenance, and cabin crews

Touchpad cursor controllers (one for each pilot) to permit each pilot to hand-control a cursor on the nav display, EICAS (for checklists), and the optional ELS side displays

Lower EICAS display for datalink interactions and for displaying synoptic graphics

Overall system fault tolerance to permit extended-range twin-engine operations (ETOPS)

Optional folding wingtips to permit aircraft access to tight gates

The 777 FBW system also includes yaw-damping capability with special gust damping for an exceptionally smooth ride. Even automatic yaw correction is provided during engine failure. The attitude-envelope protection will be in the form of high control forces when the pilot is approaching pitch and roll limits. Airspeed protection is also provided by high pitch force to limit descent pitch. Mechanical emergency backup is provided by cables to the wing spoilers for roll control and to the horizontal stabilizer for pitch control.

Another 777 innovation is the single integrated air-data and inertial-reference unit (ADIRU), which replaces three ring-laser gyro IRUs used in the 757/767. The fault-tolerant ADIRU uses six ring-laser gyros in a skewed-axis orientation to measure the three axes of rotation and acceleration. Quad-redundant processors derive the air data and inertial parameters.

At a higher level, a major Boeing innovation is the computer-aided design and computer-aided manufacturing (CAD/CAM) approach to designing and developing the 777. This is the first airplane to be designed using an advanced 3D graphics approach. The intent is to uncover and avoid manufacturing problems before the manufacturing phase even begins.

X-30 NASP (National Aero-Space Plane) and HSCT (High-Speed Civil Transport). The hypersonic X-30, to be capable of low earth orbit at Mach 25, is primarily a research project that could result in a military surveillance aircraft. The fleet of high-altitude Mach 3 SR-71s has been retired, and a replacement will be necessary by the turn of the century for military purposes. For commercial transport purposes, the HSCT program could result in a supersonic transport airplane capable of Mach 4 speeds. Other advanced commercial airplane programs are in progress in Germany, Great Britain, France, Japan, and Russia. The United States is putting a lot of resources into X-30 development, which, it is hoped, will yield an airplanelike craft that will take off from a runway, climb out of the atmosphere into low earth orbit, reenter the atmosphere, and land on a runway like an airplane.

A NASP program management office was established in December 1985 at DARPA by the undersecretary of defense and the associate administrator of NASA. In February 1986, joint program office was opened at Wright-Patterson AFB. Originally, DARPA managed the program, but the air force then took over management. Participants include DARPA, the air force, the navy, NASA, and the SDI (Strategic Defense Initiative) Organization. Major contractors include McDonnell Douglas, General Dynamics, Pratt and Whitney, and Rockwell International.

The X-30 NASP program is a high-technology development and flight-test program that may result eventually in a hypersonic vehicle that will cruise at 80,000 to 150,000 feet with a range of up to 7,000 miles. Early flight tests will probably be conducted within the speed range of Mach 5 to 15. Later testing at up to Mach 25 will accelerate the vehicle into orbit.

The HSCT will probably operate at NASP altitudes at the more efficient speed of from Mach 2.0 to 2.4. (In comparison, the well-known Concorde, which first flew in 1968 and entered service in 1975, cruises at Mach 2 at 55,000 to 60,000 feet.) At Mach 2.4, a flight from Los Angeles to Tokyo would take about 4.3 hours as opposed to 10.3 hours at sub-sonic speeds. The HSCT will not be developed for passenger use until the X-30 military-purpose vehicle is well proven. Certification will not occur before 2005.

The emphasis of this program is technology development in the areas of the airframe and drag-reducing aerodynamic structures, light-weight materials, fluid dynamics, and high-propulsion engines (called scramjet for supersonic combustion ramjet). Much has been learned with the space shuttle regarding space entry and atmospheric reentry, but much still needs to be investigated to achieve the desired single-stage-to-orbit propulsion system for a direct ascent into orbit and sustained hypersonic flight.

Supercomputers are being used extensively in the design and analysis of the aerothermodynamic aspects of the airframe and the engine. New breakthroughs in understanding these kinds of aerodynamics are crucial to the successful development of a hypersonic vehicle. Likewise, within the avionics area, development of high-performance flight control computers and sensors for high-efficiency energy management is under way. John Voelcker (1988, 32) describes the "unprecedented degree of integration," in which "the flight control computer would analyze and synthesize all input data, and send commands to control surfaces and propulsion systems to adjust angle of attack and flight path and mediate their effect on engine performance." Advances made in this area of flight control can probably also be applied to more efficient subsonic flight. Because the NASP flight profile involves both atmospheric and near-space flight, the avionics systems must be highly specialized. Certainly, sophisticated fly-by-light and power-by-wire flight control capability will be included, as well as electronic center-of-gravity autopitch control. Synthetic forward-vision capability with advanced sensors and artificial imagery will also be necessary.

The X-30 NASP is an example of the type of aircraft program that is pushing the state of the art. Robert W. Selden, chief scientist of the U.S. Air Force, stressed its importance (Canan 1989, 40): "NASP is one of our more important science and technology programs because it's pulling along so many technologies that will be really important by the middle of the next century or, with good luck, long before that."

Avionics advances will go hand in hand with the aerodynamics advances to be gained from this program.

The program has been developed in three phases.

Phase 1. Concept development (completed in late 1985) to develop baseline concepts for airframe and propulsion
Phase 2. Technology development (begun in 1986) to select airframe and engine designs and to establish technology basis for Phase 3
Phase 3. Experimental flight vehicles (begun in late 1990) to demonstrate performance and military and civil applications

Engine tests began in early 1989, and the Phase 3 decision is expected by the mid-1990s. At that time, a full-scale development (FSD) contract may be awarded to one company to build two research aircraft. The first test flight is currently planned for around the year 2000. Progress on this program is highly subject to the political and economic climate.

FSX (Fighter Support Experimental). The FSX program is a joint effort between the United States and Japan to develop and produce a fighter aircraft based on the General Dynamics F-16. A cooperative agreement was signed in late 1987. There has been much concern on the U.S. side about protecting technology interests, but proponents of the FSX program believe that the United States ought to take advantage of commercial benefits gained from involvement in the program.

The agreement between the United States and Japan ensures that the United States will benefit from technological advantages achieved by Japan, while at the same time it prevents transfer of key existing U.S. technologies. The United States hopes to acquire expertise from Japan in the composite-material production process used for the wings and advanced phased-array radar production. U.S. companies will share in about 40 percent of the development and production activity for the 100- to 130-aircraft program.

General Dynamics is responsible for the design and production of the aft fuselage and leading-edge flaps and the production of two of the first six composite wings using the Japanese curing and bonding process. Japan (Mitsubishi) has the responsibility for and will transfer technology information for the phased-array radar, EW system, inertial navigation, FBW flight control system, and fire control computer. The United States also hopes to acquire low-cost Japanese manufacturing techniques, especially for the GaAs radar transmitter-receiver modules and the co-curing process for the composite wings. If congressional approval for U.S. involvement in the program is sustained, production is scheduled to begin in 1994, with first deliveries occurring in 1999.

3.3. Spillover from Advanced Avionics Programs

Most of the programs described in this chapter are government-funded military programs. The military complex has requirements for advanced avionics capability that justify the expense of development. Often, military programs break new ground in the state of the art. These programs are often long-range, extensive research and development efforts that would be out of reach for the commercial world. However, once developed as part of government-funded programs, the resulting technology, techniques, and capability can often be adapted for commercial use. For example, the high-speed VHSIC devices, high-speed data bus, modular fault-tolerant architecture, some of the special sensor capability, and digital-map capability are all likely candidates for incorporation into commercial cockpits. In predicting future avionics capability, therefore, it is often beneficial to monitor current military and advanced commercial aircraft and avionics programs.

The transfer of lab technology to the cockpit usually follows a well-defined path. As described in the previous chapter, technological and business and regulatory forces generally preclude the radical introduction of revolutionary capability into commercial cockpits. New avionics technology and new avionics functional capability are generally the result of an evolutionary process rather than a revolutionary process. Following the evolving advances of new military avionics and aircraft programs will help the reader to stay in tune with trends.

3.4. Summary

The avionics programs described in this chapter indicate the nature of today's advanced avionics. Most of them involve advanced technology and advanced avionics concepts that in the future will be incorporated into commercial aircraft.

The military's Pave Pillar, Pave Sprinter, Pave Pace, and ICNIA programs involve highly integrated and configurable modular avionics.

The Pilot's Associate is another military-sponsored program and has as its goal employing an expert systems (ES) approach to situation awareness to provide the pilot with recommendations for action. This program avoids unnecessary automation of crew actions and removing the pilot from the control loop. The Supercockpit program involves a pilot helmet with a built-in 3D visual display system (cockpit-in-a-helmet), obviating the need for an instrument panel and its associated hardware. In this program, the pilot sees a projected instrument panel and makes switch selections via a magnetic position-sensing device at glove fingertip and by using the speech-recognition capability of the system.

Several advanced aircraft programs currently in progress include advanced avionics concepts such as flat-panel displays, fly-by-wire flight control, modular configurable avionics, speech recognition, advanced sensors, and artificial intelligence. These programs are worth watching as indicators of advanced avionics trends.

4. System-level Advances

4.1. System Integration

The development of avionics started with what might be described as a "bottom-up" or "outside-in" approach. Totally independent units were built to handle the separate functions needed, each with its own separate control and/or display: com units, various nav units, radar, autopilot, etc. Because so many separate units began cluttering the cockpit and creating a space, weight, and workload crisis, developers have tried since as far back as the 1950s to integrate and consolidate functions.

As a simple example, an audio distribution and switching panel became popular for organizing and controlling audio output from the various nav and com radios. This form of integration alleviates the proliferation of numerous kinds of different crew-interface units that have cluttered cockpits in the past. The problem with this proliferation is not just the scarcity of cockpit space but also the operational problems associated with these crew-interface differences. That is, the lack of standardization tends to slow the control process and is an opening for control mistakes and misinterpretation of information, leading to pilot-error problems. So, consolidation of operational functions within multifunction control heads or multifunction displays is one aspect of integration and operational centralization.

Another aspect of integration involves hardware integration. Whenever two or more system components are coupled by numerous interconnecting signals, it makes sense to think about consolidating the hardware. Doing this means that less hardware may be necessary and some interface circuitry and wiring can be eliminated. Duplicate hardware processing of the same data is reduced or avoided. If this fully capable central processing unit is now duplicated by a redundant backup, then the overall system functional availability is increased significantly. That is, in the event of a single unit failure, no functional loss occurs because duplicate capability exists.

Since modern avionics integration has become largely a software task as processor throughput capability continues to increase, more integration of processing functions can be achieved, resulting in savings of hardware size, weight, power consumption, etc. However, developers realize that as more information is funneled through fewer centralized processors, failures at these locations have broader ramifications. Therefore, redundancy of these centralized processors is often required to avoid massive functional failure with single-point processing failures.

This redundancy often involves exact duplicate units. However, using so-called dissimilar redundant units is another alternative that has advantages. Redundant processing units of the dissimilar kind can involve different hardware and/or different software to accomplish the same processing result. This reduces the risk of common-mode failures or algorithmic errors. The outputs of dissimilar units can be compared to detect processing discrepancies. The trend toward hardware integration, then, has the attendant risk of single-point failures creating massive loss of functionality. This reliability and functional-availability risk can be minimized with a dissimilar redundant backup unit that has the added advantage of being robust with respect to processing errors.

Still another type of integration is the sharing of data among several subsystems. For example, one air data system can provide airspeed and altitude data to several other subsystems, eliminating the need for each subsystem to have its own separate air data system. This data sharing tends to have a synergistic effect, improving the subsystem's ability to make accurate computations and to perform in concert with other subsystems.

There are, of course, pros and cons to system integration. The current choice is between a distributed system or a centralized system. This choice is not absolute. Various levels of centralization or federated distribution of functions are possible. The preference in the military avionics world is for a distributed-processing approach for combat survivability. In military parlance, however, distributed systems are typically considered bus-connected, but physically separated, subsystems. By my definition, bus-connected systems are a form of integration whereby information is shared among the subsystems integrated by the bus.

The field of avionics is still in a continuing integration period, and independent functions are being integrated through common control schemes and centralized processing schemes. There has been a natural trend to integrate more and more units into fewer and fewer central subsystems. Where centralization occurs, generally dual or triple redundancy is employed to avoid single-point massive functional failures.

This trend toward system integration and centralization has accelerated since the advent of digital avionics, and the trend is continuing, bringing these benefits:

Sharing data among several subsystems

Reducing equipment size, weight, and power consumption

Reducing the number of equipment types (Commonality and standardization of equipment is desirable for logistics reasons and for functional availability reasons.)

Locating control units in a central, easily accessible fingertip location (This drives the need for multipurpose units.)

Standardization of control and display terminology and formats for operational data, status monitoring, and maintenance data

More efficient use of cockpit panel space

Increased system reliability and functional availability

Reducing crew workload and operational stress

Multisensor data collection and correlation

System-level distributed (or federated) integration is being spurred on by modern, bidirectional, multiplex data buses, such as the MIL-STD-1553B bus in the military world and the new ARINC 629 bus in the commercial world. The military, in an attempt to standardize integration, is encouraging the standardization of processors (e.g., MIL-STD-1750A 16-bit instruction-set standard) and the standardization of software languages (e.g., MIL-STD-1815A Ada language).

Rather than being an afterthought for aircraft, avionics systems have become a major up-front consideration. The trend toward system integration has resulted in a few major focal points of subsystem centralization. For example, the flight control system (FCS) is a point of integration for air data (airspeed, altitude, vertical speed), inertial or gyro data (aircraft attitude and heading), ILS glideslope and localizer data, and radio altitude data for the coupled APPROACH mode.

Likewise, the flight management system (FMS) is a point of integration for many of these same sensor inputs and additional nav sensors and nav database data, so it can serve as an automatic lateral (route) and vertical (altitude) navigator. An FMS will typically generate an integrated display of flight route and an area map showing airports, waypoints, navaids, etc. TCAS (traffic-alert and collision-avoidance system) is already being incorporated into the FMS so that conflicting aircraft can be shown on this same display, and TCAS is also being integrated with the FCS to permit automatic expeditious execution of an escape maneuver. A weather radar display is typically also superimposed on the

FMS-generated map display to show where precipitation and turbulence are in relation to the flight route.

Where traditionally the main avionics functions were discrete com, nav, and flight control units, the trend now is for an FMS and its associated multipurpose control and display unit to centralize the management, control, and organizing of these basic functional aspects of avionics. Typically, the FMS is coupled by the pilot to drive the FCS, which in turn is engaged to control the aircraft's aerodynamic control surfaces. Because of this close relationship between the FMS and the FCS, and because of many duplicate inputs, there is a natural trend to integrate these two major subsystems into one. An example of this is the FMGCS (flight management guidance and control system) used in Airbus aircraft. The autothrottle function provided by a thrust management system, which is traditionally associated with the flight control function, is already being integrated into flight management systems. In the future, when MLS (microwave landing system) curved and segmented approaches become available, the FMS will provide the steering signals to the flight director and FCS to fly these procedures. This fosters further system integration.

The modern so-called glass-cockpit display system has been integrated so that a few multifunction displays are used to convey a multitude of information in a multiplicity of formats that can be crew-selectable. An example of the kind of integration that has occurred with display formats is the consolidation of five separate flight instruments into one display format. The standard five-instrument flight-situation group consists of airspeed, attitude, heading and navigational deviation, altitude, and vertical speed. The current trend is to incorporate all five pieces of information into one display, as shown in figure 4.1.

Integrated system monitoring automates the process of monitoring numerous subsystems and a long list of system parameters. This kind of integrated monitoring can promptly detect abnormal trends, exceedances, and other system abnormalities and alert the crew so that any detrimental effects can be minimized.

In recent years, the term *sensor fusion* has been coined to mean the integrated processing of data from an array of sensors, such as forward-looking infrared (FLIR), terrain-following and terrain-avoidance radar (TF/TA), low-light television (LLTV), radio-frequency direction-finding equipment (RFDF), electro-optic sensors, acoustic sensors, and electronic support measures (ESM) equipment. This kind of intense integration involves a massive amount of sorting, sifting, correlation, and consolidation, but it gives flight crews better situation awareness about their environment and any safety threats. The integrated information resulting is manifestly better than that provided by the individual sensors.

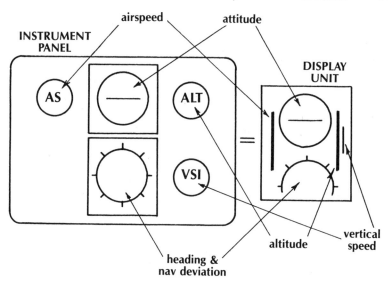

Figure 4.1. Integrated display format

Integration also provides an increased probability-of-threat detection and target recognition.

If some system information is of little value by itself, or is ambiguous, integration can enhance the system capability. Better data management through system integration increases the system's effectiveness. Integration also results in a net savings by eliminating duplication of processors, input/output (I/O) devices, databases, antennas, controls, displays, and power supplies. However, one concern that will act to slow the trend toward integration is that a fully integrated system is typically developed by a single supplier, who then has leverage over the purchaser for future maintenance, modifications, and enhancements. This situation discourages developer competition. Future integration will likely employ modular equipment to encourage supplier competition and modification flexibility. Ironically, the almost counterconcepts of integration and modularity will be very common in future avionics systems.

Currently, major guidelines for modular integration in the commercial avionics sector are being developed by the Systems Architecture and Interfaces (SAI) Subcommittee of ARINC's Airlines Electronic Engineering Committee (AEEC). Its ARINC Project Paper 651 describes a concept called integrated modular avionics (IMA). The IMA concept involves implementing avionics functionality within general-purpose processor modules. Common processing and memory modules execute avionics functions within applicable software elements. A cabinet that contains shared power supplies serves to house the modules and provides the cooling environment required. In addition to processor and power-conditioning modules, the cabinet houses memory and I/O modules with room for growth of processor throughput, memory capacity, and I/O interfaces. As far as possible, the modules are generic in their hardware. That is, there are multiple identical processor modules, memory modules, and power supplies. The I/O modules have the maximum feasible commonality, although some unique I/O interface modules will probably be necessary. Duplication of modules depends on the amount of processing throughput and memory capacity needed to perform the operational functions, the criticality of the functions themselves, and the desired functional availability.

Resource sharing is a key of IMA and serves to integrate the hardware. Multiple software elements, each one a separate avionics function, can be run on single or multiple time-shared high-throughput processors while still maintaining the required partitioning to ensure functional integrity and fault containment. Access to the processing and memory resources is efficiently controlled by operating-system software that maintains the functional partitioning of the application software. This high-integrity partitioning is expected to mean that the various avionics functions can be developed, certified, and maintained as independent elements of the integrated system.

Note that resource sharing, although making efficient use of resources, also introduces the risk that one fault may adversely affect multiple functions. Therefore, with a highly integrated shared-resource architecture, high-confidence performance and fault monitoring must be employed to detect and isolate faults. Rigid partitioning mechanisms ensure fault containment and functional integrity.

The most notable benefits of this concept of sharing processors, memory, and I/O resources are:

Improved functional performance through fault-tolerant data integration

Reduced hardware size, weight, and power consumption

Reduced number of equipment types to reduce the cost of the spares pool

Improved system reliability, maintainability, and functional availability

Improved fault-detection and isolation capability to reduce no-fault-found equipment removals (This increases the mean time between unscheduled removals (MTBUR), which translates into significant cost savings.)

The hope is that IMA will mean a reduced avionics life-cycle cost-of-ownership in terms of both initial acquisition cost and continuing operational/maintenance costs. Airplane repair turnaround time, dispatch delays, and cancellations should be significantly reduced. Furthermore, the fault-tolerance mechanisms that are expected to become an integral part of the IMA concept should permit maintenance deferral until scheduled maintenance layovers. Additionally, IMA offers potential flexibility in upgrading avionics functional capability through loadable application software while minimizing impact on the airplane's hardware.

The first real test of the IMA concept will be in Boeing's new 777 aircraft. In this aircraft, the airplane information management system (AIMS) takes a modular cabinet approach. The certification phase of this airplane, which is scheduled for delivery in 1995, will resolve the major issues associated with the integrated modular avionics architecture. The trend toward cabinet-housed line-replaceable modules (LRMs) will result in a significant reduction of the traditional black-box line-replaceable units (LRUs). What remains to be seen with the evolution of IMA is how common and standard the various modules will be. The expectation is that hardware and software form, fit, and function standards will evolve for modules. This will promote continued competition among avionics suppliers, which will ultimately result in better value to purchasers.

As mentioned, current avionics systems tend to be integrated in a distributed or federated way, with bus-facilitated data sharing. The long-term trend is in the direction of a top-down evolution, and systems will be designed to be "integrally integrated." That is, instead of integrating existing discrete subsystems, designers will look at the overall top-level requirements from the point of view of functional resources (e.g., sensors, RF stages, filters, signal processors, data processors, etc.); they will define an avionics system in terms of integrated and reconfigurable functional common modules that will be used as shared resources. These modules will have multiple duplicates for reliability and survivability, and they will be configurable on a real-time basis to perform subsystem functions, such as com radio, nav receiver, etc., as is done in the ICNIA program (see section 3.1.4). The reconfiguation will be under the control of an executive processor, which itself will have duplicate backups for functional availability (i.e., system reliability). The reconfiguration process continuously restructures the module interconnects as many times a second as necessary to meet the functional and performance demands of the situation, as determined by the flight phase and crew inputs. Constant, automatic health monitoring occurs, and when a malfunction is detected, the system's central processor knows to ignore the failed module for future system structuring. Typically, a module failure will not cause any system performance degradation. The crew will not even be aware of a malfunction, since a duplicate module will automatically take over the functions of the failed module.

An internal maintenance log will be built by the central processor. After each flight, the maintenance crew will review this log, which will indicate which modules have failed. Within a short time, the aircraft avionics system will be readied for the next flight by simple and quick module replacement. This is made possible by extensive continuous built-in test and diagnostic routines that have some level of expert system and artificial intelligence capability, resulting in a very high accuracy of isolating failed modules.

Current programs (discussed in chapter 3) that students of avionics integration trends should monitor include:

CSP (common signal processor)

ICNIA (software-intensive integrated com, nav, identification avionics)

Pave Pillar (USAF pioneer effort to integrate nav, electronic warfare, flight data, fire control, radar, and electronic support measures)

INEWS (integrated electronic warfare system, including radar and laser warning and defensive electronic countermeasures equipment)

ATF (USAF advanced tactical fighter, a next-generation air superiority fighter)

RAH (U.S. Army reconnaissance attack helicopter, a next-generation scout-attack helicopter)

ATA (U.S. Navy advanced tactical aircraft, a next-generation fighter)

The ATF program is especially important to watch for major advancements in the area of user-friendly crew interfaces. According to ATF program manager Col. Albert Piccirillo (quoted in Canan 1984, 35), "What we're aiming for in the Advanced Tactical Fighter is to integrate the man and the machine to an unprecedented extent."

Since advances in technology often support higher levels of integration, technological trends should also be monitored. Chapter 2 discussed many of the technological factors that will contribute to high integration capability. Primary among these factors are:

Multiplex data buses to simplify control and data networking (The trend is for ever-increasing bus speeds to permit simpler, more efficient and effective system architectures; the current development of a high-speed avionics data bus involves transmission rates of 50 Mbps.)

Powerful processors and special-purpose ASICs, high-density devices with built-in self-test capability and increased reliability

Standardized form-fit modules for a variety of functions to facilitate functional partitioning and support efficient logistics capability

Better high-level software languages and support tools for efficient development and maintenance

While integration results in better information and fail-safe and fail-operational capability, it does add complexity to development and testing. The complex interrelationships between integrated subsystems and/or functions often mean that more thorough testing is necessary to ensure that subtle hardware and software defects are detected. This testing may involve complex and expensive test equipment and procedures. The time required for development and testing, of course, is expanded, adding to the total nonrecurring cost of the integrated system. The trade-off, then, is that higher development cost is the penalty for the better system capability resulting from an integrated system. Again, this better capability is a combination of better information available from the system, improved functional availability (i.e., reliability and survivability), lower weight, volume, and power consumption, and so on.

As a final note on avionics integration, two other views of the integrated avionics system should also be considered. First, the integrated avionics system needs to be integrated into the vehicle within which it resides. Equipment size and weight, antenna location, cockpit layout, electrical loading, and cooling requirements are factors that must be considered. The flight control system, for example, must be tailored to the aerodynamic characteristics of the airplane and must be integrated with the aircraft's control surfaces. Also, both the flight management system and the flight control system must be matched with the propulsion capability of the powerplants.

Second, the extra-aircraft macroview should be considered. Just as avionics modules are orchestrated into a well-blended integrated aircraft system, this integrated system must also be compatible with the larger environment within which it must function. Some examples of this environment follow. In communications, future use of datalink between aircraft for collision-avoidance purposes will increase (discussed in section 7.6). Future aircraft will be more tightly integrated into the air traffic control environment using highly automated capability (described in sections 2.2, 7.2, and 7.3). On the military side, JTIDS (joint tactical information-distribution system) is a datalink scheme for coordinated communications and network data sharing. The U.S. Army's VISTA (very intelligent surveillance and target acquisition) program is intended to integrate ground forces with airborne target sensors automatically. This capability is a datalink scheme to integrate the overall battlefield activity for coordination and control from a central command position. Developers of future avionics must be concerned not only with aircraft system integration but also with integration of avionics capability with future ground- and space-based com, nav, and airspace management systems.

4.2. Automation

The rapid transition from analog to digital avionics, especially in the decade of the 1980s, and the tremendous surge of computer processing capability has made possible a high degree of avionics functional automation. That is, many aspects of flight navigation, flight control, and flight management can now be done automatically because of advances in computer-related technology. That is not to say that automation did not exist before digital technology swept the avionics field. An early example of a form of automation dating back to the 1950s was the introduction of the attitude director indicator (ADI), which in a sense automated (albeit in a mechanical way) aircraft attitude processing and presentation. The process of combining sensory information within an instrument is a form of automation. In fact, automation can include anything that alleviates the requirement for pilots to control systems manually or to process pieces of information mentally.

In the past there were dedicated full-time instruments showing sensor data. The trend now is to time-share and space-share sensor data with other data and permit the pilot to select the desired display or to display the information automatically when it is relevent. This trend is achieving a reduction of cockpit data clutter. The sheer volume of information that can be presented to flight crews is creating an information glut that contributes to pilot workload and tends to distract pilots from organizing their priorities. The increasing use of automation in the form of information management helps to decrease distractions and pilot workload.

One of the earliest examples of electronic automation was the autopilot. This avionics unit was invented out of a genuine need to reduce the pilot's workload related to maintaining a constant altitude and a constant heading. Further, when the autopilot was coupled with a nav unit, it automatically tracked a VOR radial. Automating these tasks of flying the aircraft and navigating precisely greatly eased the pilot's workload. Airplanes no longer needed to carry a navigator.

EICAS (engine-indicating and crew-alerting system) has been an important cockpit enhancement. It automatically monitors aircraft systems and consolidates crew-alerting functions into one centralized display. Another version of this is called ECAM (electronic crew-alerting and monitoring), which is used on Airbus airliners to integrate system displays on a flight-phase basis, to display checklists, and to support abnormal system management. Automation, consolidation, and centralization as exemplified by EICAS and ECAM units were key factors in eliminating the flight engineer position from many aircraft.

The rapid introduction of computer-based automation has occurred without a complete understanding of crew-machine interactive relationships. This awareness is now surfacing. The ATF program discussed in section 3.2, for example, includes avionics automation as a key issue. Some examples of future avionics automation that are being studied and developed in the military arena include the automatic planning of safe flight corridors through hostile territory, automatic terrain following and avoidance, and voice-interactive command and response capability.

The nature of future avionics depends, in part, on the relationship the pilot will have with the systems. This relationship has been in the process of changing for a long time. The current trend is for avionics to handle more and more tasks automatically without active pilot involvement. This trend toward automation is tending to remove the pilot from the control loop. It is possible, of course, to remove the pilot totally; witness RPVs (remote-piloted vehicles) and the space shuttle of the former Soviet Union. In these cases the automatic systems fly the aircraft at the datalinked direction of an external controller or by prestored mission scenarios. Some factions advocate this approach because approximately 80 to 90 percent of aircraft mishaps are due to human error (Lauber 1989). By removing this error-prone link (the pilot), we obviously decrease pilot-error problems. But there may be many more latent accidents that never happened because the pilot was there to prevent the problem. For example, if a nav radio or a circuit breaker fails, or if any number of other electronic failures occur, generally the pilot handles the problem and completes the flight safely. Another example is the not-so-uncommon situation when the pilot is presented with conflicting information from separate sources. Again, generally the pilot can resolve the discrepancy and by the process of deduction determine the real source of valid information. Brahney (1988, 16) commented on the importance of the pilot: "Studies have emphasized that the pilot has to remain 'in the loop' to maintain the required weapon system [or pilot and aircraft] performance level."

To the extent that something may reduce the pilot's workload, it also tends to lessen the pilot's control of the vehicle, and of the situation. A study done by NASA's Ames Research Center (Hughes 1989, 32) surveyed two hundred Boeing 757 pilots and reported the effects of system automation: "At least half said they felt automation actually increases workload and, one year later, these pilots showed no shift in their opinion, despite having gained more experience in the cockpit." Also, about half of these pilots felt that the head-down, hands-on avionics programming required below 10,000 feet and in terminal areas was a key safety concern. With increasing levels of system automation, pilots are relegated to only monitoring these systems. But too often, monitoring done involves head-down, hands-off activity and another safety risk.

It can be argued that automated multiple-redundant systems can error-check, majority-win, or probability-determine situations faster and more accurately than human crewmembers can. Nevertheless, this capability, when taken to the reliability levels necessary to eliminate humans altogether, is probably not cost effective. The real answer, I believe, to the pilot-elimination question will rest with what the regulatory authorities (e.g., FAA) and the flying public will find acceptable. At this point, it does not seem conceivable that passengers will ever totally accept automatic flight systems devoid of the human element, pilot error or not. The nonhomogeneous nature of the international airspace system, with its mix of nonsophisticated planes along and the very latest advanced aircraft, will preclude the far-reaching automated concepts that might otherwise be possible.

Given, then, that the crystal ball says the pilot stays, the initial question remains: What will be the relationship between the pilot and these systems? Two alternatives present themselves immediately. Either (1) the pilot will be relegated to monitoring the mostly automated avionics and handling some decision-making tasks, or (2) the pilot will actively fly the aircraft and the automated systems will monitor various flight-situation parameters for acceptability and prompt the pilot with alerts. In each case the pilot takes on the additional role of avionics systems manager. That is, the systems will have some level of automation and will perform various functions. The pilot must preprogram, select functional modes, and otherwise manage these systems.

In the case of the first alternative, when the pilot monitors automatic avionics control of the flight, the advantages are that the system can generally fly the aircraft more precisely and smoothly than the pilot can, resulting in better flight economy and passenger comfort. The biggest disadvantage is that the pilot's skills may become atrophied to a level where, in the event of an emergency or system failure, the pilot's ability to take over manually becomes lessened. This has obvious ramifications for safety. The biggest advantage is perhaps that the best use of automation is to detect and handle emergencies, such as engine failures, fires, and windshear avoidance or escape. It is common knowledge supported by "a vast literature on vigilance, as well as examples too numerous to cite . . . that the human is not a very effective monitor, and research in aviation has confirmed that when the pilot is operating in an automatic control mode, he is less likely to detect system faults than when operating manually . . . and is more likely to commit large blunders" (NASA 1988, 4). Lauber (1989, 9) points out the irony and the danger of ignoring such information: "Much has been written about people's limited ability to monitor automated systems over long periods of low stimulation. In spite of this, we continue to design cockpits which demand just such behavior from pilots. And we continue to be surprised at accidents caused by 'overreliance on automation technology.' " The trend toward automating flight functions could lead in the extreme to system capability that performs superbly under automatic control but is simply not compatible with human pilot control.

In the case of the second alternative, when the pilot takes an active role in flying the aircraft even if only on a periodic basis, the advantage is that the pilot retains a high level of proficiency and is thereby able to take over manually at any time in the event of system malfunction or flight emergency. This brings back the question of potential pilot error whenever the pilot is flying manually. However, this is where automatic monitoring capability comes into play. If the pilot should inadvertently exceed some economic or safe-flight parameter, such as forcing a rate of climb that could lead to an excessive angle of attack and a stall, the system will detect the unsafe, unusual, or otherwise unacceptable condition and alert (or automatically correct) the pilot. Two approaches are therefore possible: detection/alerting or detection/limiting. Artificial intelligence will likely be employed in the future to " 'monitor and assist rather than replace the pilot,' which could be achieved by clarifying links between man and machine including workload, awareness, vigilance, intent, and understanding, and also by developing tools to aid the pilot's interface with information and his aircraft" (Birch 1989, 40). Further, this computer-assisted flight capability will do more than just alert the pilot when a problem has occurred; it will detect trends and anticipate future problems and alert the pilot before the trend becomes a problem. Given that the pilot will remain onboard, this second alternative (hands-on, head-up) seems most probable for the pilot's role in the future cockpit. Remaining in charge and active, the flight crew will stay alert and proficient to handle situations effectively with the support of the avionics systems. The trend is for avionics designers to take a more human-centered approach to automation in recognition of the importance of tailoring avionics capability for users.

Pilots find that manually flying an aircraft is more enjoyable and beneficial to their proficiency than letting automatic systems fly the aircraft. This is especially true for takeoff and landing. There are times, of course, when engaging the automatic systems, such as flight management and flight control systems, is desirable, and pilots will do so as appropriate. To have the option of using the automatic capability is a service (almost considered a luxury) to the flight crew and is still not yet considered a necessity, except in a case like a Category 3 autoland approach, when coupling the autopilot is mandatory. J. E. Hutchinson (1989) has suggested for autoland approaches that a hybrid system composed of a normal fail-passive autopilot and head-up display (HUD) providing flight guidance cues to the pilot is a very desirable way to merge automatic capability with pilot-in-the-loop capability. As the autopilot flies the approach path, the pilot views the HUD, which displays an inertially derived flight path vector (FPV) and a runway symbol. The FPV symbol is synchronized with glideslope and localizer signals to lock on to the well-defined ILS flight path. Radio altitude is also factored in to the symbology to give the perception of moving closer to the runway. When kept involved to this extent, the pilot can effectively monitor the system's functioning and can take over immediately with no situation-awareness delay. Hutchinson (1989, 4) indicates that "the user-friendly hybrid system, which shows us how it is doing, is inherently a safer concept than the more redundant fully automatic system, which we have to trust blindly."

Determining how necessary these systems are to future cockpits depends largely on the air traffic control system. The national airspace system plan put forth by the FAA includes AERA's extensive automation of air traffic control capability scheduled for completion by about 2005. (This program is discussed more fully in section 2.2.) The program involves automatic computer generation of flight plans (correlated for collision avoidance), automatic datalinking of clearances to aircraft via the Mode S transponder datalink, and automatic enroute flow control and collision monitoring with revised clearances issued and coordinated automatically with airborne aircraft. The increasing airspace congestion and complexity of the ATC environment is demanding more flight precision, which in turn is encouraging the use of automation. As a separate issue, aircraft operators desire better route and fuel efficiency, which also points to automation as the means to achieve these goals. The major negative effect of the increasing use of automation is that it chips away at pilot proficiency and leads to the boredom in the cockpit that can reduce vigilance. This is a safety issue. These negative effects are creating a new awareness that technology should be "helping pilots use initiative and judgement, while ensuring that modern digital technology maximises aircraft performance and reliability" (Birch 1989, 39).

If the AERA concept is realized to its fullest extent, then an integrated avionics system with flight management and flight control capability becomes much more of a necessity to serve as the aircraft's point of contact with the automated ground-based control system. The integrated system will receive clearance and weather data from the ground, analyze it, prompt the pilot for acceptance or action, and then implement the received clearance. Likewise, the integrated system will monitor all flight and performance parameters, and when it determines that a different flight path or altitude would benefit performance, it will, with the pilot's concurrence, initiate automatic coordination with ATC via the Mode S datalink for a revised clearance. These are likely possibilities for onboard integrated, centralized, and automated avionics capability in the long term.

In more general terms, the potential effects of automation in industry at large continue to be debated. The issues include: (1) Will more or fewer jobs be the result of increasing automation? (2) Will productivity and economic well-being be increased or decreased? (3) Will product quality be increased or decreased? When we relate these general concerns to cockpit automation, a number of points are clear. First, the trend has been to eliminate the third pilot position because automation is performing the system-monitoring functions of the flight engineer. Second, flight productivity is being increased because automation tends to permit more precise and economic navigation with better aerodynamic performance. Finally, the product quality (in this case, flight safety and comfort) is improved because, it is argued, the automatic systems can perform more accurately with better anticipation and avoidance of flight-critical events. However, as in industrial automation, system automation in the cockpit tends to give the operator less control over the process that is automated. The extent to which this control and flight situation awareness is taken away from the pilot remains to be seen.

4.3. Summary

There is a strong trend toward achieving higher levels of systems integration and functional automation. Many benefits are derived from integrating more and more avionics functions. Common resources, such as avionics sensors and information databases, can be shared by several subsystems rather than having each subsystem provide its own resources. This eliminates unnecessary duplication of hardware and subfunction software. Integration means that more information is available for an avionics function (such as navigation), resulting in better functional performance. Better data management and improved system effectiveness are also typical results. A major benefit is a reduction of functional hardware, databases, and power supplies with a savings in weight, volume, and power consumption.

Another aspect of system integration pertains to operational areas. Multifunction controls and displays centralize and standardize systems operation. This improves operational effectiveness while also saving weight, space, power, etc., and increases functional availability through control-panel duplication.

The concept of general-purpose common modules for functional processing allows functional reconfigurability in the event of a failure. This kind of integration allows graceful degradation of avionics functionality and retention of high-priority functions after a failure.

Automation is playing an important but controversial role in the evolving field of avionics. Automatic systems can fly an aircraft more precisely and predictably than can the fallible human pilot and thus provide a more economical and comfortable ride. Automation also alleviates the pilot workload problem, which has received much press attention. The workload problem is to a large extent the result of providing too much information and capability for the pilot to handle comfortably. Informational glut and operational workload problems can lead to pilot distractions and pilot error. It is an understandable goal, then, to take advantage of automation for systems monitoring and automatic flight control. However, removing the pilot from the control loop also decreases pilot proficiency, increases pilot error potential, and reduces reaction capability, and therein lies the controversy. Total automation would require systems to be capable of dealing with all eventualities, not just foreseeable eventualities. Human pilots are naturally inventive and therefore much better able to deal with the unforeseeable situations. It has been noted also that human pilots avert more system-caused problems than they cause. The ultimate potential danger of automation is an automated aircraft that operates beautifully and efficiently under automatic control but is so aerodynamically unstable or so complex that it cannot be controlled by the human pilot. This sets the limit for systems designers and for automation.

5. Crew-System Interfaces

5.1. General

Crew-system interfaces are those controls and displays that the crew uses to control and to receive information from the systems. I am assuming that for the foreseeable future a human crew will remain on board and in control of commercial aircraft systems. According to Stefan Geisenheyner (1989, 64), however, in the military air-combat arena "it is not all that fanciful to imagine that the large majority of tactical combat aircraft of the next century will be flown without either pilot or cockpit. Even so, there will always be certain missions for which a human in the cockpit is essential."

This chapter describes the trends related to the interaction of flight crews with avionics systems. The principal crew-system interfaces are the displays on which the pilot views information about aircraft flight attitude, nav data, weather radar, systems status, etc. The trend is to make more use of multipurpose displays. That is, various informational displays are selectable by the crew. Different display formats are time-shared on the display units as desired, depending on the informational needs of the crew. This permits reversionary display of information on another display unit in the event of failure of the primary display unit. Other crew-interface topics discussed include interactive speech recognition and synthesis, spacial auditory cueing, and trends in switching technology. Untapped human sensory capabilities are being studied for possible inclusion in future cockpits. The final topic has to do with the important area of operational simplicity.

Designers follow certain fundamental rules when developing system interfaces for flight crews.

The information presented and the control selections provided must be useful and necessary; anything else should be automated or deleted.

The information presented and the control selections provided must be intuitive; otherwise they are a workload issue, and any resulting misinterpretation or misunderstanding can lead to misuse and detrimental effects.

The information presented and the control selections provided must have consistency within the overall interface environment; otherwise unintentional misuse can again result.

The trend indicates that future avionics will likely conform to these rules more closely than they did in the past.

5.2. Multipurpose Units

To reduce the number of controls and simplify pilot workload, many avionics manufacturers have produced keyboard units that serve as input devices for multiple subsystems. These keyboard units are usually full alphanumeric keyboards, but generally they are not configured for optimized text entry (i.e., not QWERTY keyboards). Also, multipurpose displays permit the crew to select the desired display format from an available menu. Normally, the keyboard and display units are packaged together. An example of a multipurpose control display unit is shown in figure 5.1.

The value of these multipurpose devices is that they serve as the crew-system interface for several subsystems, thereby obviating the need for separate dedicated interface units. In addition to saving weight, power, volume, and panel space, these multipurpose devices serve to standardize the method of subsystem control. That is, the pilot knows from a top-level menu or set of function keys how to gain access to a desired subsystem. Having accessed that subsystem, the pilot views another menu and selects a control function. In this way, the pilot can quickly go from top-level subsystem selection to lowest-level mode activation, frequency selection, etc., in just a few keystrokes, and can do it in a consistent, standardized way. This kind of control-unit commonality and resulting operational standardization also would support a common type-rating for pilots. That is, for different airplanes with very similar cockpits and operational procedures, such as the current generation Boeing 757 and 767 (Boeing 707/720 and Convair 880/990 from earlier generations), a pilot who is licensed to fly one will be approved to fly the other with minimal additional training.

Figure 5.1. Multipurpose control display unit (photo courtesy of Smiths Industries)

Each crewmember who has one of these multiple-redundant input and output units has control over the entire system. In the event of a single control-unit failure, no operational function is lost, since it is still controllable from a redundant unit. That is, multiple-redundant control units increase overall system reliability (functional availability) and survivability by virtue of their multiplicity. Each crewmember can be provided with the same kind of control unit that gives access to all functions.

It is worth mentioning that the centralized control scheme is not without its drawbacks. Access to a particular function may be confusing and difficult. For example, a sequence of menu selections may extend so far down into nested page displays that a person can have difficulty remembering how to get to the desired page. The scheme itself must be very intuitive so that the operator knows exactly how to reach the desired goal. The more functions and subsystems that are accessible through this centralized control unit, the bigger the problem. One can usually solve the problem, however, through a careful approach to the page layout and information on each display and to the sequence of button-pushing leading from one page to the next and back. The lack of standardization of these aspects adds to the cost of ownership (e.g., training, manuals, etc.) for operators with different equipment in the same fleet.

5.3. Displays

Since the first introduction of the electronic flight instrument system (EFIS) at the beginning of the 1980s, more and more aircraft are being outfitted with these versatile CRT displays as opposed to single-purpose electromechanical instruments (figure 5.2). The so-called glass-cockpit capability is the current trend in avionics displays (figure 5.3). By about 1995, the CRT displays will begin to get serious competition from solid-state flat-panel displays (see section 2.3.1).

When planning the development of crew-system interfaces, designers must know the kind of information a pilot needs and when it is needed. Data should be displayed at the right time and otherwise removed to avoid clutter and reduce crew workload. *Situation awareness* is the phrase used to describe the need pilots have for information related to the aircraft flight and nav situation. Avionics developers have responded with a heightened interest in presenting information to flight crews in ways that facilitate situation awareness. A great deal of effort is being put into military programs such as ATF, RAH-66, and Supercockpit (discussed in chapter 3) to improve pilot's situation awareness. This is

Figure 5.2. Older complex cockpit (photo courtesy of NASA)

very important in the military arena because flying in combat is an extremely stressful environment, and military aircraft have numerous electronic warfare systems providing critical flight-safety and threat-advisory information. Good information management is imperative. The results of research and experience in these military programs will eventually spill over to commercial avionics systems. There is a clear trend toward improving crew-system interfaces and operational simplicity.

The trend for future avionics is toward more use of electronic displays because their formats can be readily reconfigured for particular situations. For a given display format, the information presented and

Figure 5.3. Modern airline cockpit, Airbus A330/A340 (photo courtesy of Airbus Industrie)

the symbology used can be optimized for the situation, and any unnecessary clutter can be removed from the display altogether. Color is already widely used to code information. This has the visual effect of decluttering displays. That is, it is easier to find or understand the information presented if it is color-coded. For example, information displayed in red is normally considered critical, high-priority information that the pilot needs to be aware of and deal with immediately. Other display trends include larger displays (10-inch-square flat-panel displays are being considered for the long term) and higher resolution for better clarity.

EICAS (engine-indicating and crew-alerting system) displays are an example of the flexibility provided by glass-cockpit capability. The EICAS display presentation includes parameters from aircraft systems, such as engines, fuel, hydraulic, pneumatic, air-conditioning, electrical, and pressurization. The parameters can be shown in conventional circular formats, vertical formats, and/or digital readouts. These and other systems parameters are monitored for exceedances and trends. Crew-alerting messages are generated and displayed on the EICAS display in color coding to inform the crew of critical (red) situations and caution (yellow) conditions. System status (white) annunciations are also displayed for the crew's information. EICAS displays can also present color-coded system schematics (called synoptics) to show the crew in a pictorial form where a system problem exists. This kind of display format achieves a high level of intuitive system situation awareness. Checklists may also be called up on EICAS displays. The crew can sequence through the list by carrying out the appropriate action to confirm each item. Color coding is used to indicate completed items, the current item, and the next items. As the checklist progresses, relevant subsystem synoptic drawings can appear automatically to provide intuitive confirmation of proper system response.

Other kinds of displays are being evaluated for more extensive use in cockpits. For example, head-up displays (HUD) are used in military cockpits, particularly for combat purposes (figure 5.4). A HUD is also being used in some commercial cockpits today to ease the transition from the instrument approach phase to the landing phase. Alaska Airlines, for example, began using HUD technology in the mid-1980s. Enhanced vision imagery is being planned for inclusion with HUD presentations (see section 6.5). However, a persistent major problem with head-up displays is that they are monochrome. Color can be very important in the support of situation awareness. Moreover, a HUD really does nothing to alleviate the pilot workload problem, although it helps the pilot keep a head-up attitude and look out of the cockpit, rather than down at cockpit systems. Nevertheless, as Graham Warwick (1988, 23) said, "the head-up display is on the way out, it seems, at least in the fighter cockpit." Warwick also said that "in the quest for wider and wider fields of view, attention has switched to the helmet-mounted display (HMD), which always puts the information right where the pilot wants it, in front of his eyes."

Helmet-mounted displays are being considered in military cockpits to give the pilot better situation awareness. Military research labs are going so far as to portray three-dimensional panoramic views on instrument panels and within helmet display systems. Virtual images of the outside world give pilots a much better spatial feel for their flight and mission situations, as compared to information from basic instrument-panel displays. The symbology of head-up display capability can be incorporated in the pilot's helmet visor so the pilot sees the information no matter which direction he or she is looking (figure 5.5). The helmet would have orientation sensors that permit the pilot to cue onboard sensors such as radar, threat-warning electronics, and collision-avoidance sensors. The collision-avoidance system could also cue the pilot via

Figure 5.4. Modern military cockpit, Mirage 2000-5 (photo courtesy of Sextant Avionique)

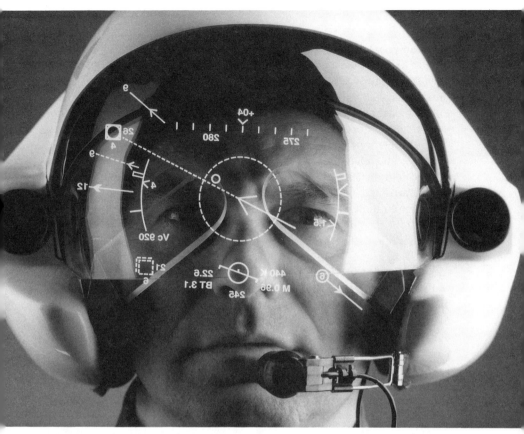

Figure 5.5. Helmet-mounted display (photo courtesy of Sextant Avionique)

helmet visor symbology to look in the direction of the potential threat.

The Supercockpit program, described in section 3.1.6, is an excellent example of the highly integrated crew-interface capability of the future. The pilot wears a helmet with built-in sophisticated audiovisual capability. The built-in display projects images of the outside world with relevant superimposed symbology to cue the pilot's situation awareness to mission-critical situations. The three-dimensional stereo sound system also alerts the pilot to outside threats, such as attacking aircraft or missiles, and to the direction from which they are coming. If eventually adapted for commercial use, the helmet system could alert the pilot to potential midair-collision threats, obstacles during approach and departure, ground proximity, etc., in addition to providing a clear outside view even if poor weather conditions exist. The aircraft's sensors will have the ability to "see through the fog" and, therefore, enhance situation awareness and flight safety.

Lap projection units are being evaluated to give military pilots a so-called God's-eye view of a battle area from 20,000 feet up. Holography is in the early study stage for possible further use in future cockpits. Computer-generated holographic imagery is already being introduced into military cockpits, and Warwick commented on it (1988, 23): "Developments such as holographic optics have met the demand for increased field-of-view for night flying and target indication." A three-dimensional situation awareness image would give the pilot information on potential ground and air threats.

A program conducted by the Naval Air Systems Command called Command Flight Path Display (CFPD) involves using an aircraft outline on a flight display. The pilot flies in a wing position to the displayed command aircraft. The command aircraft symbol even includes graphics for landing gear, speedbrakes, and tailhook to prompt the pilot to extend these at the appropriate times. "Highway-in-the-sky" graphics are used to depict the desired route of flight. The pilot need only fly the aircraft along the depicted flight path and follow the cues provided by the command aircraft graphics. Flight attitude, direction, and speed are properly achieved by matching the command aircraft. Flight tests of this capability were completed in 1988 and were considered successful: "These flights validated the pictorial display as an effective flight guidance tool, which enabled pilots to consistently fly successful operational Navy missions under instrument meteorological conditions (IMC)" (Scott 1989, 51).

Digital map display capability has been developed and continues to be improved as technology advances are being made. One military program is called STARS (stored terrain and access retrieval system). In this system, terrain data for four million square nautical miles are stored in a digital database and can be retrieved for display. The terrain display presentation includes full-color perspective views. This capability can be used for nap-of-the-earth terrain flying, target acquisition and weapon delivery, and autonomous navigation. These kinds of display systems, currently being pushed within the military arena, will eventually be adapted for use in commercial cockpits.

Currently, a great deal is being done to use graphics processing to advantage in future cockpits. As graphics technology advances, particularly with virtual three-dimensional and stereographic presentations, cockpits will see a slow maturing of this capability.

5.4. Speech Recognition and Synthesis

Speech synthesis is the use of humanlike voice phrases generated by an electronic system to inform the crew of a condition that typically has imminent implications. These voice phrases are usually repeated twice in sequence. Generally, the crew needs to respond to this kind of alert immediately to resolve the condition that triggered the alert. An example of a speech-synthesized alert is "pull up, pull up," which is used to alert the crew that the airplane is too close to the ground. The F-15 uses "over-G, over-G" during high-G maneuvers to warn the pilot of possible blackout or airframe overstress problems. This F-15 alert is generated in a female voice as an attention-getting mechanism. As a rule, synthesized voice is used in cockpits today to get the crew to respond to urgent situations such as ground proximity, windshear, and other flight-critical threats. In the future, speech synthesis may be a method of soliciting information from the flight crew to provide the automated systems with needed data.

Speech recognition is the system capability of identifying a spoken word or phrase from the crew. This capability will make it possible for the crew to interact with onboard systems in a more natural and immediate way and will facilitate control actions, especially during times of high workload and high stress. The crew might also use voice command for checklist actions, weather data requests, operational data requests, nav profiles, datalink message transmission, weapons aiming, target priorities, and frequency and mode selection.

Sophisticated speech recognition depends on neural-networklike AI (artificial intelligence) pattern recognition with adaptive learning capability. Currently in its infancy, speech recognition depends heavily on tremendous processing throughput (hundreds of MIPS). Future speech recognition systems will be able to recognize a large vocabulary (tens of thousands of spoken words and phrases) even under different conditions of voice pitch and timbre. One goal is to achieve speaker-independent, continuous-recognition capability as opposed to the more limiting speaker-dependent, discrete word–recognition capability. Future heuristic interactive speech capability will be able to deal with a range of equivalent phrases, for example, *two-niner-niner-two* versus *twenty-nine ninety-two*. Today's limited speech-recognition capability must necessarily restrict recognizable grammar. In the long term, grammar restrictions will be reduced as natural language understanding is incorporated into speech-recognition systems.

Voice-command and voice-response capability will reduce the need for other time-consuming, head-down crew-interface devices, such as keyboard units. However, there could be significant differences in applying this technology in cockpits with single versus multiple crews and between civil versus military operations. Also, in some cockpit environments that are far less sterile than others, nonpertinent conversations could create unexpected and undesirable responses from the speech-recognition system.

5.5. Directional Sound

Currently, tones, bells, and horns are used to alert pilots to various conditions, such as low airspeed, gear-up, and other abnormal conditions. These sounds are not intuitively associated with their respective conditions, however, and can even be more of a distraction than a helpful alert. Pilots must learn what the sounds mean. One possibility for improving this deficiency is using three-dimensional sound, which cues the pilot to look toward the source of the sound. Humans can discriminate sound direction to within 3 to 4 degrees (Dornheim 1986, 115). Future cockpits will employ this method along with speech synthesis and aural alerts to help cue crewmembers to the direction requiring attention. Three-dimensional sound helps pilots locate external threats or prompts them to focus on a cockpit control panel or display for critical information.

5.6. Switching

Traditionally, avionics switching has consisted primarily of dedicated switches (e.g., push-button and toggle-action switches). Future switching will likely involve more multipurpose menu-selection switching, often as part of the display system. Much of the switching activity will involve crew control of the display cursor. The operator will place the cursor over or next to a menu item for selection. Control of the cursor can be done using mouselike devices, such as a trackball, joystick, strain-gage sensor, or finger-sensitive touchpad.

Keyboards may also become more prevalent. Membrane and conductive-rubber technology may outpace traditional hard-contact push-button keyboards. Display touchscreen capability is also appearing in cockpits because it facilitates better crew-system interactive switching. Touchscreens virtually eliminate the need for physical keyboards because the keys can be called up on a display whenever needed. When the keyboard is not needed, the display can be used for other purposes. Icon symbology is becoming more popular too, especially in conjunction with touchscreens. Icons represent functions in a direct intuitive way rather than using multiple-word explanatory phrases. The biggest risk is the problem of using symbols that have no intuitive meaning. In these cases, they defeat the purpose of using icons and create a workload problem.

Push-button switches with programmable legends may be used more in the future. The avionics system can prompt the pilot with information and recommended actions via the switch legends, and the pilot can make a switching selection, as desired. The concept of a "dark and quiet cockpit" will become more common in the future; that is, systems status will be monitored by exception, and information will be displayed only on condition. Generally, switch legends will be unlit until an action is required by the crew. The lighting of a switch legend will serve as a prompt to the pilot to perform some action. Fred George (1988, 103) discussed the advantages of switch legends: "Normal operations are characterized by an absence of extraneous distractions. Rather than having a large number of normally idle annunciations and warning lights, most warning and advisory functions pop out as messages that interrupt and overlay normal CRT displays."

The concept of virtual switches associated with the military's Supercockpit program was described in section 3.1.6. Virtual switches are projected images of switches that appear only when desired or some switch action is required. When the pilot reaches out to "touch" the projected switch image, a position sensor in the glove fingertip feeds the fingertip position back to the system. When the fingertip is in the vicinity of the virtual 3D position of the switch image, then the system activates the switch. A tactile feedback mechanism in the pilot's fingertip provides the pilot with the sense of touch pressure.

Another part of the Supercockpit program is the capability for a pilot to activate a switch simply by looking at it and issuing a voice command or pressing an activate button. The helmet contains a mechanism to detect the pilot's head orientation and eye direction. This capability is important in high-G maneuvering when arms and hands are virtually immobile.

Research is currently being conducted to develop what could be called gesture-recognition capability. This involves special computer-interfaced spatial sensors that permit the recognition of hand and finger orientation and motion. Outside the field of avionics, so-called virtual tools are being developed to achieve highly accurate remote shaping, smoothing, etc. For example, in some cases the worker cannot directly manipulate an object because it may be too large, too hot, or too heavy;

virtual tools permit remote manipulation of the object. In avionics this kind of capability could conceivably be used in future cockpits to permit control of the aircraft through virtual control devices. This would make flexible control possible without involving the weight, mechanical linkages, or wiring associated with physical controls.

5.7. Operational Simplicity

I am including operational simplicity in a section of its own because of its importance in the design of modern cockpits. In this age of computer capability, designers can provide vast amounts of information to flight crews. The hard part is managing this information so that pilots are not flooded with data to the point of overload. Information management involves the use of automation to process sensory information, consolidate it, and filter it as part of a data-reduction function. Another function of information management involves presenting information only when it is relevant or only upon demand. Pilots generally want information only in the amount or to the degree needed at the moment. They must absorb a piece of information, decide their response and take action, and then absorb the next piece of information. This is a continuing iterative process. A third function of information management is presenting information in an intuitive format to alleviate the pilot workload problem. It is this third area that is receiving intense scrutiny. For example, an analog readout may be best for a changing parameter (e.g., altitude during descent) and a digital readout is helpful when a parameter must be maintained (e.g., altitude during straight and level flight).

Future avionics will emphasize an intuitive interface between the human pilot and the avionics system. In the past this interface consisted of switches, knobs, dials, indicators, and so on. Each of these control interfaces had a dedicated purpose to permit the pilot to activate some function or to give the pilot some indication of flight or system status. Although these controls may have been labeled, they lacked real intuitiveness as to their purpose within the context of the flight situation. The proliferation of dedicated interfaces has led, in some cases, to a severe overcrowding in the cockpit and a detrimental workload factor for the crew. The Pilot's Associate program described in section 3.1.5 was conceived as a solution to the problem of overloading fighter pilots with information and system-management tasks.

Avionics capability needs to be both functionally useful and operationally simple. In a sense these two requirements are contradictory because usefulness leads to more and more functions, which lead to more and more operational complexity. A compromise needs to be made. While functional usefulness is desirable, it may result in operational aspects that are very complex. Likewise, if the operational aspects are made very simple, the functional usefulness may be reduced too much. Once the tradeoff is resolved, the keynote of any good crew-system interface is operational simplicity. That is, the crew operational interface should be as simple and as intuitive as possible.

There are also the factors of consistency and flexibility to consider. Consistency in the basic control approach to several subsystems avoids confusion. Flexibility in the interface lets the pilot achieve a control objective in multiple ways. Still, the overriding goal is to make the interface simple and intuitive. When activating a mode or setting a code, the pilot should not become confused or slowed down because of the difficulty of interpreting prompts or analyzing decision points.

Avionics developers are making significant strides in simplifying cockpits and pilot workload by reducing the numbers of switches, knobs, indicators, controls, and dials. For example, the early Boeing 747 had 971 controls and indicators, whereas the 1988 version 747-400 has only 365. The average two-crew jet transport has on the order of 450. Similarly, the DC-10 had around 1,000 controls and indicators, but the next-generation MD-11 has only around 300. This reduction of controls and indicators can be misleading, however, because many modern controls and indicators are multimode in nature, requiring the user to be familiar and adept with the many possible modes.

While it is preferable to simplify the operational aspects of an avionics system, in the process the pilot may be denied access to manual control of certain functions. If these functions are better done by automatic systems and there is no need for the pilot ever to intervene, then fine. If, however, the pilot may need to control the function manually on occasion, then loss of this access is detrimental.

To further illustrate the workload problem, consider the F-18 fighter. It has three primary displays on which 675 acronyms can be displayed at various times along with as many as 177 different symbols (in four different sizes) in any of 40 different display formats. Additionally, there are 73 advisory messages that may appear on these same displays. Elsewhere in the same cockpit are 59 indicators, and the HUD has 22 different display formats. The throttle lever contains nine switches (mostly multifunction) and the control stick contains seven switches (Geisenheyner 1989, 52). The systems have created a training and workload problem for the pilot, especially in a combat environment, when "what the combat pilot urgently requires is the automatic display of pertinent information in simple and clear format, and only when it is actually needed" (Geisenheyner 1989, 54).

The trend toward reducing the numbers of controls and indicators has centered partly on automating certain avionics system functions and partly on providing functional access to the pilot via a centralized crew-interface system, such as a control-display unit or a multifunction display.

Another area of operational simplicity involves selecting the correct kind of control (e.g., toggle switch, twist knob, push button) for the particular function or mode actuation. Some operational modes are more intuitively handled by one type of control. For example, the gear-up/gear-down switch is intuitively controlled by a lever that moves up and down. Some controls can be problematic in nature, such as a twist knob to control vertical speed. Should a clockwise twist cause a nose-down attitude (higher-descent vertical speed) or should it cause a nose-up attitude?

Achieving operational simplicity and helping crews manage workload involves several factors:

Automating fixed-response actions

Eliminating secondary information from the displays when not needed

Using intuitive display formats, such as virtual three-dimensional representations of flight path

Annunciating message text, illuminating panel bulbs, and directing aural alerts only when action is necessary; otherwise these distractions are extinguished

Eliminating false-alarm annunciations

Using intuitive symbology to convey information to reduce interpretation time

Using symbology that differs in at least two parameters (e.g., size, color, shape)

Using consistency in symbology color, such as red for critical alert, green for active modes, white for scales, etc.

Pilots are trained to scan instruments rapidly while picking out pieces of relevant information. This rapid scan permits the pilot to control the airplane's flight attitude, to navigate precisely, and to otherwise manage the flight situation. Ironically, as Oliver Shearer III (1986, 102) pointed out, scanning has become more difficult: "In the past, the indicators have been needles, tapes, or other analog devices. Digital information slows down the scan, forcing one to read and process every number. Sometimes, just looking at relative positions of old-style indicators is all that is required in order to keep up with flight and engine instruments."

Although the new electronic glass-cockpit displays are able to paint multicolor situation formats, movement away from the traditional flight-display formats, such as the artificial horizon and compass card, has been slow. The traditional artificial horizon, or attitude director indicator (ADI), presents a view that simulates looking forward at the earth's horizon; it shows the airplane's attitude—pitch up or down and wing bank or roll. The compass card view, or horizontal situation indicator (HSI), presents a look-down view; it shows the aircraft's heading and navigational course-deviation information. In both cases the information is presented as a two-dimensional view, one looking forward and the other looking down. To complete the three-dimensional picture, the pilot must mentally integrate more information, factoring in (1) altitude information from the altimeter and vertical speed indicator and (2) forward progress information from the airspeed indicator along with groundspeed from available nav units. This mental picture of the flight situation is, therefore, a composite puzzle image developed by correlating several one-dimensional and two-dimensional pieces of information.

For intuitive situation awareness, the two-dimensional map display mode was introduced with the 1982 Boeing 767 to help the pilot see the navigational situation (i.e., where the airplane is in relation to airports, navaids, waypoints, and programmed flight-plan route). Also, the weather radar display can be superimposed on the map display to give a visual indication of where the weather is in relation to the route and airport. At some point in the not-too-distant future, situation displays will have more intuitive presentations of virtual three-dimensional perspective views or stereographic three-dimensional presentations. This will alleviate some of the pilot's mental workload and give a more complete and direct display of flight situation (e.g., aircraft attitude, present position, and navigational status and progress).

Situation displays are display formats that are tailored to a specific situation to help the pilot intuitively understand the situation and thereby know the best way to deal with or control it. An example is the landing approach, such as an ILS or MLS approach. A desirable display for this situation would be a perspective view, or a virtual three-dimensional display, to show the lateral and vertical approach path as viewed from the aircraft's present position with respect to the desired path. This would make the glidepath intercept and tracking an intuitive exercise. Currently, pilots must interpret needle indications that reflect two-dimensional (up/down, left/right) situations and then integrate these indications mentally to understand the three-dimensional situation. A head-up display achieves some degree of improvement over conventional displays in this regard. Situation displays present relevant flight and mission situations and cue the crew to high-priority actions with symbology or voice alerts.

As an example of what has been done to simplify operations, EICAS (engine-indicating and crew-alerting system) will display alerts and warnings only when they are active; otherwise the system status is not presented, thereby decluttering the display. If pressures and temperatures are within normal tolerances, they are removed from the display. On transport aircraft, David Hughes says (1989, 34), "the number of warnings a pilot has to cope with—has been spiraling up to 400–500, and EICAS simplifies things by reducing the number on the Boeing 757 to below 200." Another example is the Boeing 767 overhead panel, which has normally unlit switches. However, when parameters require some pilot action, the relevant switches light up, cueing the pilot to the necessary action.

Predictive information displayed for pilots contributes to intuitive understanding of flight situation. For example, an airspeed trend arc on the airspeed indicator can be used to show what the airspeed will be in ten seconds. This gives the pilot an intuitive cue as to how quickly airspeed is increasing (or decreasing) and how soon a critically high (or low) airspeed might be reached. Likewise, a trend vector for altitude can show what the aircraft's altitude will be in thirty seconds. Symbology can show if a waypoint crossing restriction can be met, or symbology can show predictive flight path over some future time, such as thirty seconds, sixty seconds, etc.

We are beginning to move into an era when flight operational information such as navigation charts and aircraft performance data will be stored and accessed electronically rather than in paper manuals. Recent advances in optical, magnetic, and solid-state memory-storage capability permit onboard storage of massive amounts of information. With steady advances in database management capability and superprocessing capability, the idea of a "paperless," or at least a reduced-paper, cockpit is coming closer to reality. High-resolution display of flight and maintenance information with rapid search, scrolling, browsing, panning, zooming, and random access will bring another wave of massive data infusion into the cockpit. There will be attendent challenges in managing this information in a user-friendly way without creating more workload problems.

As more and more capability is built in to avionics systems, there is necessarily more and more for crewmembers to know to be able to operate the systems and understand the information available from the systems. They need to understand the various operating modes, combinations of settings, and indications. So, as more functional capability is provided to the crewmembers, they are taxed with more workload. One solution to this problem is to automate as many functions as possible, as discussed in section 4.1. There is a tradeoff involved, since automating a function removes control authority from the crew. For example, automating the turbine starting sequence means that an engine can be started by a simple push of a button. However, under certain circumstances, this automatic sequence may fail to start the engine (e.g., if the pneumatic start valve fails). In such a case, the pilot could have success with access to each step in the starting sequence. On the other hand, of course, knowing exactly what to do, when, and how much, can be a workload problem.

In many cases, the automatic and manual modes are selectable at will and the pilot has the best of both worlds. Flight control is a good example. If the pilot desires to fly a route manually, the flight control and flight management systems are simply not used. If the automatic capability is desired, a flight route can be programmed into the flight management system and coupled to the autopilot. This kind of crew-system interface flexibility is desirable and, no doubt, will continue to be available in future avionics.

The system automation capability currently available, coupled with intuitive crew-system interfaces, is making possible two-pilot crews on modern airplanes, such as the Boeing 757, 767, 737-300, and 747-400; the Airbus A330 and 340; and the McDonnell Douglas MD-11.

Future avionics will make use of expert systems (ES) capability and artificial intelligence (AI) to simplify cockpit workload. An "expert" database can be used to aid onboard fault isolation in highly integrated systems. This database will emulate the thought process of a highly experienced line-maintenance technician who follows a logic fault-tree process that is based largely on past troubleshooting experience. An ES approach can also be used to handle critical inflight emergencies, such as engine failure on takeoff. Again, the ES capability emulates the actions of a highly qualified expert pilot with very high accuracy and quick reaction time. Artificial intelligence will be used because of its adaptive learning capability. For example, AI capability can store aerodynamic efficiency data under varying flight conditions. Based on this data, subsequent flights under the same conditions can be optimized for better aerodynamic and engine efficiencies. Refer also to sections 3.1.5 and 3.1.6, which describe military AI capability in the Pilot's Associate and the Supercockpit programs. ES and AI will be used more in future avionics to supplement pilot situation analysis and provide decision-making assistance. ES and AI will thus simplify operational tasks while improving flight capability.

Future avionics systems will also include embedded training and help functions to facilitate initial and recurrency training in real time and in flight. As technological advances permit higher levels of system integration, the additional capability resulting from avionics has the potential of overwhelming the operator. One of the biggest challenges is to make systems more easily usable as more capability is added. Avionics can no longer be designed without regard for the human operational aspects.

One current concrete example of the strong interest in improving the crew-system interface is the U.S. Army's MANPRINT (Manpower and Personnel Integration) program, which the army is applying to the RAH-66 helicopter program (see section 3.2). The concept behind MANPRINT is to optimize a system for human usability, including pilots, maintenance, and logistics personnel. The motivation for MANPRINT has been the army's experience with modern sophisticated systems that tend to suffer from a lack of user-friendliness. The army feels so strongly about the user-interface issue that about 30 percent of the selection score for the RAH competitors was based on their MANPRINT evaluation.

5.8. Summary

Modern avionics is vitally interested in human factors, the way human pilots relate to electronic systems. Crew-system interfaces in the past have led to pilot workload problems when too much information was presented, resulting in clutter. Some crew-system interfaces have also involved too much operational activity for the pilot to access the information. Multipurpose controls and displays are becoming popular to centralize the location of the crew-system interface and to standardize the control and display methods and informational formats. This consolidation of many separate control panels and displays into a unified multipurpose control-display unit has the added benefits of weight, volume, power, and panel-space savings.

One frequently used term in modern avionics capability is *situation awareness*. It refers to the ability of onboard systems to give the crew information about their flight, mission, and systems status. Onboard systems should provide situation awareness and have the following attributes:

Color-coded displays
Decluttered display formats that provide information when and

where it is needed
Intuitive display presentations
Menu selection of control options
Interactive voice-command and voice-response capability
AI/ES situation analysis and decision aiding

Crew-interface advances currently being developed and refined for cockpit use include:

Helmet-mounted displays that keep information always in front of the pilot's eyes
Graphics display capability for more intuitive presentations
Digital map capability that shows the pilot where the aircraft is in relation to flight-plan route, navaids, terrain and obstacles, other air traffic, airspace restrictions, significant weather, etc.
Speech recognition so the systems can accept pilot commands and queries directly to permit a more natural and immediate interaction between the pilot and the systems
Directional sound cues to focus the pilot's attention in a specific direction or on a particular control unit
Virtual switches (projected switch images that appear on an imaginary panel for a pilot to "touch")
The concept of a dark and quiet cockpit in which annunciations are turned on or alerts are sounded only when crew attention and action are required

One of the biggest challenges for modern and future avionics systems is achieving operational simplicity. As avionics systems permit more and better functional capability, it is almost a necessary evil that more workload and operational complexity results. In the future, judicious use of human-centered automation will be used, where appropriate, to help crews manage workload. Also, attempts will be made to present information intuitively and only when necessary.

6. Navigation Advances

Although many independent navigation systems in use today will continue for several years, the FAA's national airspace system plan and its successor, the aviation system capital investment plan, indicate that some of these systems are headed for phaseout. For example, the 1987 national airspace system plan stated that ILS would be phased out over the period 1995 to 2000 (although in recent years this projection has softened significantly). In addition, according to the DOT/DOD Federal Radionavigation plan (see Lowenstein et al. 1988, 17), "Military support and use of TRANSIT, LORAN-C, Omega, VOR/DME and TACAN will be phased out," except probably for shipboard use. However, this phaseout will occur only if the global positioning system (GPS) (see section 6.2) becomes operational as an approved sole means of navigation. ICAO (International Civil Aviation Organization) currently requires the continuation of VOR/DME until 1995, but it is likely that ICAO will extend the phaseout to the year 2000.

6.1. Historical View

The trend in navigation in the past was to conceive new systems that provided some aspect of operational capability not previously available. Early nav systems were based on low-frequency ground-transmitting beacons. Aircraft receivers provided information to the pilot regarding where the plane was in respect to the beacon and which way to fly to home in on the beacon. In the early days, the pilot listened over headphones to signal tone and strength. The very early low-frequency four-course radio beacon was developed by the Ford Motor Company and first activated in 1927, during the heyday of the Ford Trimotor. These beacons gave way to high-powered nondirectional beacons (NDBs), which were really all-directional beacons. By 1965 the high-powered enroute NDB navaids began to be decommissioned, but low-powered NDBs remain in use as low-cost nonprecision systems. In the cockpit, the receiver for early NDBs involved a manually rotated loop antenna and a radio compass display. In time the aircraft antenna rotation was automated and the receiver system became known as the automatic direction finder (ADF). The ADF was the first nav display to make use of an arrowhead automatically pointing toward the NDB station.

The VOR (VHF omnirange) system came into existence during World War II and was officially adopted as the national civil navigation system in 1946. It is still the primary system for cross-country radio navigation today. VORs have more reliable signals and permit much more precise nav capability than NDBs do.

The military's TACAN (tactical air navigation) system is like the VOR but operates in the UHF spectrum. It also includes ranging capability for use with the onboard distance-measuring equipment (DME) that became available in the early 1960s for nonmilitary use.

Other systems are also in use today, such as LORAN-C and Omega for long-range navigation based on ground-transmitted signals. The inertial navigation system (INS), also called inertial reference system (IRS), is an onboard, self-contained system that determines position information based on integrated aircraft accelerations. Doppler nav systems make use of the well-known frequency-shift effect that occurs when a signal is transmitted from a moving vehicle and is reflected back to its source at a frequency difference proportional to the vehicle's velocity with respect to the ground. Another navigational system called TRANSIT uses a satellite-borne transmitter and vehicle receiver that is also a Doppler system but requires very sophisticated data processing to extract vehicle velocity and position. RNAV ("random" or area navigation) came into vogue in the early 1970s and is based primarily on processing VOR and DME information from multiple VOR/DME stations. RNAV systems provide point-to-point nav capability by establishing artificial waypoints that, in effect, electronically reposition VORs to new locations along the desired flight-plan route.

A significant navigation advance currently being phased in involves satellite-based navigation, or satnav, capability (described in section 6.2). The global positioning system (GPS), developed by the United States, uses several satellites in orbit. The aircraft GPS receiver determines its three-dimensional position from these satellite-transmitted signals. This satnav capability has the potential of virtually revolutionizing onboard nav capability and, in the long term, will likely make obsolete many of the systems currently in use. Although the military is expected to adopt GPS as soon as possible and to phase out Omega by December 1994 and TACAN by December 1997, the civil and international aviation community will continue to use existing nav systems until GPS is well entrenched, proven, and cost effective.

Meanwhile, some existing systems, like LORAN-C, will be improved to serve their purposes better until satellite navigation is mature. Currently, the DOD intends to phase out LORAN-C by December 1994. For civil purposes, however, LORAN-C, whose LORAN-A ancestor has been around since 1940 for marine uses, saw an explosion of popularity for aircraft use in the 1980s. LORAN-C has a good chance of significantly increasing its nonmilitary use until well into the next century because it is sufficiently accurate and inexpensive. In a very real sense, LORAN-C has revolutionized the nav capability of general aviation aircraft by providing a low-cost area-nav capability to this aviation community. Another new nav capability called the microwave landing system (MLS) may also greatly facilitate navigation for terminal arrivals. MLS is described in section 6.5.

Historically, then, several systems have come into use and have evolved to provide different ways of giving position and ground-track information. So far, new systems have proliferated without making older systems obsolete. Many aircraft are equipped to use one or more such systems. Most of the existing systems, however, will be phased out over time when GPS becomes widespread.

6.2. Satellite-based Navigation (Satnav)

GPS (global positioning system), often called Navstar (navigation by timing and ranging), is a satellite-based navigation system. Satellites in orbit provide information to onboard GPS receivers that triangulate the receiver's position with respect to these satellites with a high degree of accuracy. Since the satellites' instantaneous positions with respect to an earth-centered coordinate system are also known, the receiver's three-dimensional position and position change (velocity) are determined with respect to the earth's center. For aircraft equipped with a GPS receiver, the aircraft's position, groundspeed, and altitude above mean sea level are computed without using ground-based nav sources and without using pressure-sensitive air data systems. GPS positioning accuracy is independent of the distance between the receiver and the satellites, unlike many existing ground-based nav systems.

The implementation of early satnav systems dates back to 1963, when the navy used its own satellite system called TRANSIT (first used in 1964 and released for nonmilitary use in 1967). The navy also had another satnav project called TIMATION in progress. In the early 1970s the air force also had plans for developing 3D satnav capability called 621B. The GPS concept took form April 17, 1973, when the navy and air force were directed by the deputy secretary of defense to join forces to develop a single satnav system that became known as GPS or Navstar. The first prototype GPS satellite was launched on February 22, 1978. By about 1994 the complete satellite complement will make GPS fully operational for civil use.

Design position accuracy for military GPS systems with precise positioning service (PPS) is 16 meters which is about 52 feet. In testing, precision positioning accuracy ranges between 2 and 15 meters (Nordwall 1988, 83). Commercial GPS systems with standard positioning service (SPS) have a design accuracy of about 100 meters (325 feet) horizontally and 170 meters (560 feet) vertically. Standard positioning accuracy has been measured at approximately 40 meters. Velocity accuracy is 0.1 meters per second and clock-time accuracy is 100 nanoseconds. This kind of accuracy has the potential to revolutionize how we navigate. That is, with the advent of GPS, vehicle navigation is becoming less dependent on earth-bound transmitting systems, which are more subject to atmospheric propagation aberrations.

Satellite navigation provides worldwide common-grid coverage over mountainous regions, deserts, oceans, and everywhere else, including remote polar regions. Since GPS receivers can be used in conjunction with an extensive database containing geographic, terrain, and obstacle data, full RNAV capability with enhanced ground- and obstacle-proximity warning capability is not far off. It is easily conceivable that GPS can be used not only for enroute navigation but also for approach navigation, thereby obviating the need for most ground-based approach systems, as discussed in section 6.5. Also, satnav capability can improve airplane collision avoidance and ground and obstacle avoidance. For example, for two or more aircraft equipped with GPS, their relative positions and closure rate can be determined accurately by a highly precise common-reference satnav system. Likewise, an onboard terrain and obstacle database could permit this kind of collision avoidance.

Eighteen satellites 10,900 nautical miles high in six orbital planes (three satellites per plane) were originally planned to be operational by 1989; however, the space shuttle *Challenger* disaster in January 1986 caused a delay. GPS should become fully operational as a supplementary civil satnav system by the mid-1990s. With complete satellite coverage, from six to eleven satellites will be continuously visible to any GPS receiver anywhere in the world. Four satellites are required for a GPS receiver to compute 3D position because very precise time (the fourth parameter) is an essential element for the computations. Three-satellite coverage will permit determination of two-dimensional position (latitude and longitude). A fourth satellite will allow determination of altitude as well. If a fifth satellite is receivable, ionospheric conditions can be computed to improve system accuracy.

The original plan was to have a constellation of eighteen active satellites. However, in certain areas and at certain times GPS coverage would be degraded. That is, either four satellites would not be in view at all times, or two or more might be in a spatially disadvantaged relationship, reducing nav accuracy. Therefore, the FAA could not approve GPS as a sole means of navigation: "For GPS to become a sole means for civil aviation (for oceanic en route, domestic en route, terminal and nonprecision approaches), at least five satellites must be in view above a mask angle of ten degrees, where all combinations of four out of five satellites have 100-meter accuracy" (Federal Radionavigation Plan—Part 2 1988, 10). GPS would be approved as a supplemental system when used in conjunction with, for example, INS or Loran-C.

A total of twenty-four satellites (twenty-one plus three spares) is anticipated by 1994 to complete the GPS satellite constellation. This full complement of satellites is still not sufficient for sole means approval without additional integrity enhancements, such as fault monitoring and detection capability, to warn users of degraded satellite capability. Central system monitoring with a GPS integrity channel and autonomous receiver built-in detection schemes have been proposed and are being considered.

The former Soviet Union's satnav system GLONASS (global orbiting navigation satellite system) is very similar to GPS. Its first satellite was launched on October 12, 1982. Like GPS, when GLONASS becomes fully operational by the mid-1990s, its space complement will consist of twenty-four satellites. The GPS and GLONASS satellite systems have different orbits but both provide global coverage. It is likely that the United States and Russia will work together to share satnav resources in the spirit of a U.S.–Soviet agreement signed in May 1988. It is expected that by the mid-1990s a combination of forty-eight GPS and GLONASS satellites will be operational in orbit, providing worldwide, continuous, full-capability satnav service. This means that at least twelve satellites will be visible to any hybrid GPS/GLONASS receiver anywhere in the world. Since GPS and GLONASS involve dissimilar techniques for position determination and since each system is independent and operated by independent agencies, satnav could achieve sole-means-of-navigation status through U.S.–Russian cooperation by 2005 (FAA 1990, 1-0-16). The system availability requirement could be met because of the number of satellites GPS/GLONASS will provide. The availability of more satellites also means that a better geometric configuration could be chosen by the receiver, allowing GPS/GLONASS to meet the accuracy requirement. The integrity requirement might be met either by (1) mechanisms added to the satellite system to provide timely fault warnings, or (2) comparison computations performed by GPS receivers. The U.S. military is planning on phasing out its use of VOR and TACAN by the year 2000 and using GPS as the sole means of enroute navigation.

In addition to providing nav capability, GPS can compute an aircraft's pitch, bank, and heading. It measures the phase difference of the carrier signal received by two antennas placed, for example, at the wingtips. Bruce Nordwall (1991, 72) indicates that "if four GPS satellites are visible, it is possible to determine the three-dimensional vector from one antenna to the other with accuracy less than a 0.1 meter."

Other kinds of satnav systems are in the feasibility phase. The journal *Avionics* (October 1988, 12) stated that "developments in technology appear to justify the prediction that global navigation satellite systems (GNSS) that provide 'independent' onboard position determination will evolve as sole means of navigation, and eventually replace current navigation aids." Western European countries have considered developing a satellite navigation system that serves their region. The European Space Agency (ESA) has proposed a system called Navsat. In addition, Germany has a concept called GRANAS (global radio navigation system). These or other satnav systems will evolve to displace most existing navigational systems.

In another form of satellite navigation under consideration, multiple satellites determine the range to aircraft with a ground-based system computing the aircraft's position and transmitting this information to the aircraft. This form of satnav is not receiving general favor, however, because its interdependent nature reduces overall reliability. The communications link from the ground to aircraft would be critical, a safety implication that is unlikely to be overcome.

It has been predicted (Eydaleine 1988, 17) that in the longer term "satellite navigation systems could replace all conventional radionavigation systems, which would enable the ground infrastructures to be abandoned, since they are very costly in investment and maintenance." It is too early still to estimate when this might happen because several factors are involved, including technical, business, political, and user-acceptance issues. Agencies such as ICAO and the FAA must also approve GPS before it can become the predominant means of navigation. GPS acceptance will likely occur over a transition period of at least fifteen years as costs decrease and user confidence increases. A stumbling block for nonmilitary GPS users is the Defense Department's "selective availability" control, with which it can degrade positioning accuracy. This problem will likely be resolved in future negotiations or by U.S. governmental decision.

The Future Air Navigation Systems (FANS) committee of ICAO is developing a somewhat generic specification to facilitate intersystem satnav compatibility. Both GPS and Russia's GLONASS satnav systems meet the accuracy requirements of the FANS specifications.

6.3. Inertial Navigation

Although GPS is likely to change future navigational capability permanently, it will not make all existing onboard nav systems obsolete. There is much to be gained from integrating GPS with inertial nav capability. For example, GPS can calibrate INS with drift rates, and INS data (attitude, accelerations, and heading) can aid GPS. GPS interferometric measurement of pitch and roll attitude and heading can also be correlated with INS attitude and heading measurements.

Practical inertial-gyro autonavigator capability originated in the early 1950s with floating gyros. This technology evolved by the early 1970s to dry gyro systems that were smaller, lighter, more accurate, and had shorter alignment times. After about twenty-five years of laboratory research, in 1975 Honeywell developed the ring-laser gyro (RLG) that was later introduced into the new 757 and 767 aircraft. RLG systems have an order-of-magnitude better reliability (on the order of 7,000 hours MTBF due to no moving parts), reduced power consumption, immunity to G forces, and reduced alignment times. Like conventional INSs, RLGs measure roll, pitch, and yaw rates while eliminating the moving mechanical parts, such as gimbals, torquers, slip rings, and resolvers.

Over this inertial gyro evolution, position accuracy remains somewhat constant at about 1 to 2 nm per hour with velocity errors of 5 to 10 knots. It is possible, however, for highly accurate inertial systems to achieve 0.1 nm per hour accuracy. The BAe LINS 300 laser gyro system (see Marsh 1987, 25) "computes position to one nautical mile (drift) per hour, velocity to 2.5 ft/sec (horizontally) and 2 ft/sec (vertically), heading and attitude to 0.1 degree, and measures turn rates of up to ±400 degrees/sec. Alignment times are 1.5 minutes for stored heading and 4 minutes for gyro compassing." The technology is state of the art, according to Marsh (1987, 26): "a laser gyro the size of a microchip . . . has been developed by Bodenseewerk Geratetechnik (BGT). This 'laser on a chip' gyro will be ready by the mid-1990s, says BGT."

Inertial nav has good short-term accuracy but naturally degrades over time and requires periodic corrections. Typically DME distance data from multiple DME stations are used to correct inertial platform drift and improve position accuracy to about 0.2 nm per hour and velocity error to 0.5 m per second. DME is not available on transoceanic flights. In the future, GPS will be used with inertial systems as a hybrid combination to take advantage of GPS's long-term accuracy and the inertial system's aircraft attitude and short-term accuracy data. Integrating the highly accurate GPS precision position data with an inertial reference system "enables inflight calibration of inertial platform velocity errors to be achieved with a medium-term (i.e., a few minutes) accuracy which can be measured in centimetres per second" (Condom 1987, 852).

6.4. Terrain-referenced Navigation

Terrain-referenced navigation involves the use of the radio altimeter (in conjunction with barometric altitude) to obtain a ground contour map. This map is then compared with an onboard terrain database that contains a 3D terrain model. Using a nav system such as INS, starting from a known location and moving in a known direction, the system continuously searches for terrain database matches to keep track of position. The accuracy of the method depends on the database's digital resolution of terrain data points. Sweetman and Hewish (1988, 38) state that "when an accurate fit is found, the aircraft's position is known, typically to within 10–15 m." This accuracy is used to continuously calibrate the INS to eliminate its long-term accuracy degradation.

This navigation method is particularly useful for military applications, such as terrain following and terrain avoidance (TF/TA). Other valuable applications include ground proximity warning and precision "highway-in-the-sky" flight path navigation. This method, of course, is independent of ground and space nav systems. It requires powerful processing capability, however, especially during erratic maneuvering.

The military also uses a high-resolution ground-mapping radar system known as the APG-70. This is a Doppler-type nav system that is used in conjunction with an INS to factor out velocities and accelerations from the ground map.

6.5. Terminal-area Navigation

The FAA plans that the automated enroute ATC (AERA) program will permit an increase of air traffic densities in the enroute flight phase (see section 2.2). Some scheme must therefore be used to increase traffic densities during the arrival terminal-area phase, which is the primary bottleneck in the airspace system. The microwave landing system (MLS), which was first proposed by ICAO in 1972 and selected as an international standard in 1978, is billed as the solution. The DOT, DOD, and NASA, under FAA management, along with Australia, jointly developed the MLS concept. MLS in its fully developed form will permit simultaneous reduced-spacing approaches to parallel runways using straight, curved, or segmented paths (see figure 6.1). This capability will permit multiple aircraft to simultaneously transition from the enroute phase (20,000 feet and 20 miles out) to the instrument-approach arrival phase on precise paths that are optimized for their direction of arrival. Less air-traffic-sequencing delay during this transition will result, and therefore more traffic will be fed more efficiently from the enroute phase to landing.

MLS is more reliable than ILS, which was introduced in 1947, since it is less susceptible to propagation disturbances caused by snow buildup and soil moisture or by vehicle and building perturbations. Currently all MLS Category 1 approaches permit a decision height of 150 feet with 1,600-foot runway visual range. The standard ILS Category 1 approach, by comparison, is limited to a 200-foot decision height and a 1,800- or 2,400-foot runway visual range. Lower approach minimums permitted by MLS result in increased traffic arrival flows and reduced flight delays.

The ILS system has a total of twenty 100-kHz internationally authorized channels available and consists of localizer and glideslope signals providing single-direction precision approach capability for landing aircraft. By contrast MLS has two hundred channels and provides precision position-locating capability and approach flexibility in a volume of airspace at the approach end of a runway. This airspace volume is provided by the MLS transmitter, which sweeps a lateral beam plus or minus 40 degrees (a few will be capable of plus or minus 60 degrees) from the extended runway centerline and sweeps a vertical beam from 0 to 30 degrees above the horizon up to 20,000 feet AGL and extending to a distance of 20 nm. MLS coverage will generally be limited to plus or minus 40 degrees in azimuth and 1 to 15 degrees in elevation.

The onboard MLS system with suitable nav capability can be programmed to display course guidance for the selected flight path. This path can be programmed to be straight, curved, or segmented to avoid

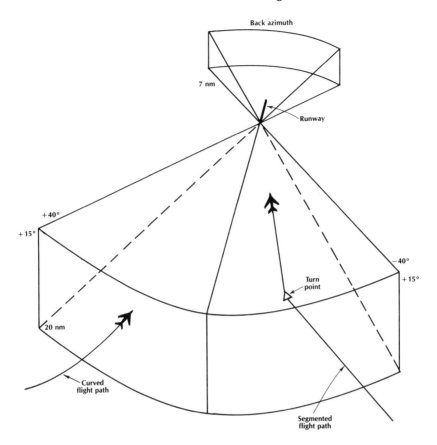

Figure 6.1. Microwave landing system

obstacles, cities, etc. A flight director system can be used to display the flight situation in terms of lateral and vertical deviation from the programmed approach. MLS curved approaches will probably require EFIS display to give the pilot confidence that the system is flying the prescribed approach properly. Precision DME (DME-P) capability will also be available with selected MLS installations to provide distance and progress information during the approach. DME-P will be used in place of the ILS marker beacons. This capability will permit aircraft to plan approaches from various directions and alleviate the current situation, in which all aircraft intercept the same approach path. The result will be more efficient use of terminal airspace to expedite inbound traffic and thereby relieve the congestion of terminal areas. Harry Hopkins (1988, 24) reports that "MLS, with turn-ons at 4 nm at all four airports [in a 20-

nm radius complex of New York and New Jersey], would give benefits equal to one whole new airport."

As with new avionics, the existing ILS system will remain in place during the phase-in of MLS. Currently ICAO requires the continuation of ILS until the year 2000 and will likely extend the phase-in period. This will permit aircraft operators to remove the older ILS equipment as it ages and install new MLS equipment. By January 1, 1998, MLS is planned as the ICAO standard precision-approach aid at international airports. At a point when most aircraft are MLS-equipped, the ILS system will be officially terminated. By 2004 the FAA plans to have 750 MLS systems collocated with existing ILS systems, with 500 additional new systems installed. Military phase-in of 400 to 500 MLS systems is expected to begin in the 1990s and be completed by 2003.

The FAA ordered MLS equipment in January 1984 for airport installation, and the first delivery was received in mid-March 1988. The schedule for MLS phase-in, however, is largely subject to user acceptance. Many users are resisting MLS now because of the expense, since they feel that the existing ILS serves them adequately. The FAA argues forcefully that by the turn of the century the existing ILS channel availability will be bankrupt and unable to support air traffic growth. The FAA also cites air traffic delays, airport congestion, and the need for increased terminal arrival capability. Europe seems more committed than the United States to the phase-in of MLS. European countries are planning to equip most of their major airports with MLS before the mid-1990s.

Over some years, then, MLS could replace ILS as a precision-approach aid. However, with improvements in ILS reliability (from solid-state digital technology) and with a decrease in ILS siting problems, ILS is now looking more competitive with MLS, which may delay the widespread introduction of MLS until some extended future date. Whenever GPS is considered for application as an approach aid, it will initially phase in for non-precision-approach use. In any case, a more efficient transition from the enroute to the approach phase will be provided, thereby facilitating more efficient takeoff-to-landing traffic flow.

In the long term GPS might be used with a suitable nav system to permit straight, curved, or segmented approaches, but from an onboard satellite receiver system without the need for the ground-based MLS transmitter. Although GPS is not officially intended as an approach aid, a method called the differential technique (or just differential GPS) could be used to make GPS very precise for approach purposes. This technique requires that another GPS receiver be fixed at a precisely known ground location at the airport of landing. This monitor unit can determine the differential GPS range error of the received GPS signal because it knows its own correct position. The error amount is then real-time datalinked to the onboard GPS system to correct its calculations for precision-approach guidance. Using this method, a pilot can achieve position accuracy of 75 cm to 5 m. In flight testing conducted early in 1991, as Bruce Nordwall (1991, 72) reported, "differential GPS gave a position with a cross-track error of 0.1–0.9 meters, and vertical accuracy of 0.8–3.3 meters." Another possibility involves a ground-based, simulated GPS satellite that can correct for a poor GPS satellite geometry. This "pseudosatellite" could transmit the error data without having to use a datalink.

The onboard GPS-based system could include a database with the prescribed approach paths for each airport. With knowledge of the approach path and with precision GPS nav capability, the onboard system could fly an approach without reliance on ground-based guidance signals. A question still to be resolved is whether GPS-based guidance can meet the requirements for category 2 and 3 approaches (see table 8.1). A major argument against using GPS for arrival navigation is the military control of GPS and the possibility of its degrading GPS accuracy during national emergencies. GPS positioning update rates and failure modes also need to be studied for their effects on GPS accuracy and integrity.

The cockpit use of millimeter-wave imaging radar for scanning the ground ahead of the landing aircraft facilitates better approach flow and landing certainty. This sensor cuts through low-visibility conditions with a range of at least one and one-half miles. An image of the ground, obstacles, and airport ahead is projected so the pilot can "see" the runway environment. A forward-looking infrared (FLIR) sensor can also be used to provide better night vision. According to FAA HUD project manager Malcolm Burgess, "Infrared has better resolution but range and contrast are strongly affected by humidity and thermal conditions. Millimeter-wave radar has poor resolution but is less affected by bad weather. Its range is limited to several miles with current technology. The present plan is to switch between sensors, but a next-generation system could create a single image by combining sensor inputs (Dornheim 1992). A synthetic vision system (totally artificial image) or enhanced vision system (includes outside visual images) processes the sensor data and generates an image for display on a head-up display (HUD). Also appearing on the HUD are aircraft attitude, altitude, airspeed, and heading. This gives the pilot much better head-up cues for landing. In a way, we are coming nearly full circle in the history of navigation. In the early days pilots depended heavily on visually determining their location by observing landmarks. Today advanced synthetic-image sensing helps pilots to "see"—and safely complete—approaches, landings, taxiing, and even takeoffs. Established nav guidance is still required for approaches, but visual imaging could permit safe operations in lower weather minimums. Enhanced vision capability may allow Category 1 and 2 instrument approaches (see section 8.5) when the weather is below normal minimums for these approaches. That is, Category 3 approaches could potentially be accomplished using runways authorized originally for Category 1 or 2 approaches.

Over the next decade a visual approach guidance system using laser beams may gain more favor. This capability has been in use in the former Soviet Union since the beginning of the 1980s. Although the laser beams can be seen through poor visibility for about two miles, lack of electronic coupling with onboard systems will limit its widespread use.

On the airport grounds, future high-speed runway turnoffs onto taxiways will make possible more closely spaced arrivals. If Category 3 landings (see section 8.5) become more common for reduced-weather landings, electronic taxi guidance would also permit airports to accept aircraft for landing as fast as approach facilities can deliver them. Future hybrid nav systems that combine the attributes and accuracies of differential GPS, ring-laser gyro technology, precision accelerometers, and airport map displays may evolve to provide onboard guidance capability for taxiing in low-visibility conditions.

Although this section emphasizes arrival navigation and the potential for MLS and GPS to expedite this phase of flight, I should mention that MLS and GPS may also play an important role in facilitating the initial departure phase of flight, primarily because they permit precision flight navigation in the terminal area. MLS and GPS can do for the departure and arrival flight phases what RNAV has done for the enroute phase.

6.6. Airmass Navigation

Traditional navigation generally has involved flying cross-country from one navaid to another at a fixed altitude that tries to take advantage of prevailing tailwinds or at least to minimize headwinds. With RNAV capability, cross-country navigation can be done on a direct route from the departure point to the destination, and again at a generally fixed altitude. The concept of airmass navigation involves flying a path of least airmass resistance, taking into account the real-time existing air density and currents. This means that the flight path will meander laterally and vertically.

This concept is at radical variance with the current method of air traffic separation, which depends primarily on fixed lateral flight paths and vertical altitudes. Pilots already take advantage of some of the principles of airmass navigation (tailwinds, for example) to the extent that they have knowledge of the airmass they are flying in and to the extent that ATC can grant requested altitudes and routings. These are currently the limiting factors, since pilots have limited real-time knowledge of the airmass and ATC can grant requests on a traffic-permitting basis only.

The airmass tends to have continuous, smooth changes in temperature, pressure, and density with transitional boundaries at the airmass fronts. Within a given airmass, pressure gradients vary vertically and horizontally, forming the shape of the airmass. Today, aircraft are assigned to lateral flight paths and fixed mean-sea-level altitudes without regard for airmass shape. Because of this, aircraft cut across the pressure gradients and plow through the airmass without taking advantage of the natural air-flow patterns.

Of course, taking advantage of the natural airmass flow patterns requires knowledge of these patterns, and these patterns move along with the airmass, which is itself in motion. Ultimately, an aircraft's integrated avionics system must receive external meteorological information on a real-time update basis, must process this information with respect to the aircraft's present position and known flight-plan route, and must compute a changing lateral and vertical profile to plan a path of least resistance from present position to destination. This external real-time information can come to each enroute aircraft in the following way. First, the air data system senses air pressure, temperature, density, and motion for the parcel of airmass it is currently in. This information from each aircraft is relayed to a central databank using a datalink. The central databank builds a composite large-scale picture of the airmass structures over wide areas. Continuously updated meteorological information relevant to each aircraft's flight route is then uplinked to each aircraft. Using this information, the aircraft's central avionics system directs its flight-control system to fly the path of least resistance.

This process of determining the path of least resistance might be accomplished more efficiently by high-capacity, ground-based mainframe computers that not only have access to the airmass structures databank but also have knowledge of all the aircraft positions. With this additional information, the mainframe computers can determine efficient airmass flight paths that also preserve collision avoidance for all aircraft. Furthermore, since the traffic-flow congestion occurs mostly at terminal areas where the traffic converges for landing, the mainframe can plan flight paths that efficiently transition the aircraft from the enroute phase to the arrival phase while simultaneously optimizing flight paths for airmass efficiency and ensuring collision avoidance.

6.7. Radar

Radar systems are not traditionally considered conventional nav systems, but radar is used as a very important source of flight information to help pilots determine where to go or where not to go with regard to weather. Therefore some of the advances in airborne radar systems are important to navigational trends.

For navigation, weather-detection and turbulence-detection radar are more important than the military radar applications, such as air defense surveillance, reconnaissance, fire control, or airborne early-warning radars, although many advances are taking place in this arena as well. For example, radar functionality has been improved by bistatic radar capability (in which a separately located transmitter and receiver permit covert tactical operations) and over-the-horizon (OTH) capability (which detects targets up to 2000 nm away). Radar technology has also been advanced by improved antennas (which have phased arrays with ultralow sidelobes) and by solid-state implementations (e.g., MMIC integrated technology for improved reliability, maintainability, and lower size and weight; solid-state amplifiers that replace klystron tubes; and VHSIC and VLSI technology for high-performance signal- and signature-processing capability).

During World War II, scientists developed radar primarily as a ground-based early-warning system to detect enemy aggression. They quickly realized that ground-control radar could provide safer navigation for aircraft at night, in inclement weather, in fog, etc. Not until the mid-1950s, however, did radar equipment become small enough and light enough (still several hundred pounds) to be practical for airborne use. The employment of transistor technology in onboard radar systems in the mid-1960s finally made it feasible to equip small-cabin aircraft with weather-radar capability. Flat-plate phased-array radar antennas became available in the late 1960s to improve focusing capability and transmitting efficiencies over parabolic dish antennas.

The first digital radar equipment (the Bendix 1200) was introduced in 1972. Although it was monochrome, it greatly improved the display of weather echos. Multicolor presentations clearly showing intensity gradients began to appear in the late 1970s.

Rockwell-Collins introduced the first turbulence-detection radar capability in 1983. Doppler frequency shifts caused by water-drop acceleration differences represent areas of turbulence. In the fall of 1987, Collins introduced a new Doppler radar that operates well with very low transmitted power (24 watts, as compared with the typical several thousand watts). The radar uses gallium-arsenide (GaAs) devices that are six times faster than ordinary silicon chips and permit a processing speed of eight million instructions per second. High-performance statistical signal-processing techniques can detect very faint echos in the low-power radar returns. The highly stable solid-state transmitter and sophisticated receiver signal-processing capability permit low-power radars to operate. Low weight (seventeen pounds), smaller size, and low heat dissipation are also associated with the low-power advantage.

Weather radar systems are being included in the trend toward functional integration. In aircraft with EFIS display systems, flight routes can be superimposed over the weather radar depiction so that pilots can view weather and turbulence in relation to their routes. New weather radar systems may also be able to detect and display microburst and windshear activity in time for the pilot to avoid hazardous encounters, as described in section 8.6.

Artificial intelligence (AI) capability is also important in relation to weather radar systems. The AI function will evaluate pertinent variables to determine whether a weather threat exists. Patricia Rickey (1987, 40) explains: "Theoretically then, when confronted inflight with potentially severe weather, a pilot could signal the computer (presumably by some key stroke or touch function) to look into the situation. He could then forget about it because the computer would automatically check the radar, consult a realtime weather information service, process the variables, conclude a 'best choice' response, display the choice, and instruct the various aircraft systems to make the changes necessary to avoid the troublesome weather cells." Weather radar capability, then, is an important support tool for navigation.

6.8. Summary

Many nav systems still in use today were conceived during World War II to increase the utility of military aircraft. VORs, for example, still dominate international navigation. Likewise, transponders for ATC radar identification originated out of a wartime need to be able to identify friend or foe (IFF) aircraft.

Area navigation, a major advance of the early 1970s, permits point-to-point direct navigation based on VOR/DME capability. LORAN-C has long been used for maritime navigation, but since the mid-1980s it has had an explosion of use in aircraft. We are now nearing a major advance that makes use of satellite-based nav signals. GPS promises to virtually revolutionize worldwide navigation in the 1990s. At some point, most nav systems in use today will be phased out as GPS and other satnav systems mature.

Satellite navigation is particularly useful in support of the enroute flight phase. The microwave landing system (MLS), while still uncertain and controversial, is planned to support navigation during the arrival flight phase. Future MLS capability will permit curved, segmented, and straight-in approach paths to selected runways. This will facilitate better ATC sequencing and separation of arrivals while improving terrain and obstacle avoidance during approaches. A "differential GPS" method is another way of obtaining precision-approach nav capability. This method is likely to be introduced at some major airports in the late 1990s.

Also important for the future is airmass navigation, the concept of flying an aircraft along the path of least airmass resistance. This is a very long range possibility and requires onboard knowledge of airmass currents. This information, presumably, would be datalinked from an ATC databank to aircraft on a virtual real-time basis. The databank would be continuously filled by information provided from enroute aircraft based on their actual airmass measurements. For airmass navigation to be successful, advanced collision-avoidance techniques would also need to be developed. Admittedly futuristic in concept, airmass navigation indicates what might be possible rather than what is actually planned.

7. Communication Advances

7.1. Introduction

The potential for avionics communication was demonstrated in 1910 when, according to Daniel Holt (1985, 12), "a radio was used to transmit and receive signals from an aircraft . . . the first official use of an avionics-type system in an aircraft." HF com radios were the mainstay until World War II when VHF com radios were developed. Most transport aircraft carried radio crewmembers until their positions were phased out in the 1950s. Advances have been made in VHF equipment over the years, but now we are on the threshold of significant changes in the area of aviation communication. This chapter discusses:

1. *Trends in air-ground coordination.* These include traditional ATC and company communications currently accomplished via voice. I also describe the Mode S datalink and satellite com capability.
2. *Trends in data communication other than air-ground coordination.* These include interaircraft transponder-conveyed information, such as collision-alerting and collision-avoidance messages.

Note that transponders and collision-alerting equipment are included in the category of communication. This is an unconventional association since transponders traditionally have been considered a totally separate category. Moreover, collision-alerting systems are still new, and their function does not fit conveniently into either the com or nav category. I place transponders and TCAS (traffic-alert and collision-avoidance system) in the com category because transponders *communicate* information to and from ATC and TCAS communicates information between aircraft. The information is not the traditional kind of voice-coordination information, but its communication is relevant to flight safety in this era of higher-density traffic. In this sense transponders and TCAS fit well into the com category.

As might be expected, the digital avionics revolution is sweeping the communication systems area. Even aircraft audio systems are employing a digital approach to improve sound quality, equipment reliability, and selftest capability, as well as to reduce wires, weight, and cost.

7.2. Air-Ground Coordination

Pilots use the guideline "aviate, navigate, communicate," to establish their cockpit responsibility. Note that *communicate* is considered the third priority. That is, pilots should first fly (attitude, heading, altitude, airspeed, etc.) the airplane safely, then navigate (determine position and maintain course), and finally communicate flight information as necessary. Communication in today's ATC environment mostly involves acknowledging information or clearance receipt from ATC or requesting altitude or route changes, all voice requests in a somewhat standardized format.

Although considered of lessor priority than flying the aircraft and navigating, communicating is still an important and necessary pilot function. The consequences of poor communication are well known. Much has been said and written in the literature about poor voice-communication technique, including procedures, enunciation, and phraseology. In today's high-density terminal areas, poor technique can not only slow traffic flow but also cause misinterpretation that leads to in-flight conflicts. Misinterpretation of voice communication can result from poor voice technique or from improper readback and acknowledgment.

Approximately 80 percent of flight problem reports cited by pilots are related to oral communications. It is usually in the busiest of traffic situations, when good communication is most necessary, that communication breaks down. This happens because there is little time for analyzing, understanding, or clarifying voice transmissions. International language differences and concise ATC phraseology also contribute to problems. Poor headphones, speakers, or microphones may cause communication breakdown, and the sheer time required for voice transmissions leads to frequency congestion. Because of such problems with voice communication, datalink capability promises to become more prevalent in future avionics.

In North America, the airlines (represented by Aeronautical Radio, Inc: ARINC) already have an existing nationwide VHF-com network dating back to 1977 for company data transmissions. Called ACARS (aircraft communications, addressing, and reporting system), the system was conceived to permit airliners to transmit free or formatted text messages and digital data back to their company facilities. This information includes gate-out and gate-in times, takeoff and landing times, flight progress, maintenance requests, engine data, weather information, etc. As an example of increasing efficiency, ACARS automatically transmits a "landing touchdown" signal. The signal alerts ground personnel to be ready to handle the arriving flight and minimizes turnaround time.

The airline dispatch center could use ACARS to transmit ATIS (automatic terminal information service data), flight plans, weight and balance data, weather data, etc., to their aircraft. Other possibilities for ACARS uplink include the transmission of weather turbulence plots, terminal radar plots, and ground terminal maps. Downlinks from aircraft include system diagnostics data for loading into a history databank.

Future ACARS use may include computer-to-computer data transfer. For example, real-time engine data could be datalinked to a central computer for analysis. Datalinked system information allows preventive maintenance to reduce mechanical failures and aircraft downtime. This desire for datalinking more and more system and operational information has spurred a new bit-oriented data transfer protocol called AVPAC (aviation VHF packet communications), which is compatible with open systems interconnection (OSI) standards. AVPAC and ACARS use the same OSI physical layer, at 2,400 bits per second. ARINC is currently developing an AVPAC ground network.

With the advent of satellite communications, ACARS and AVPAC are likely to employ this capability to improve and maximize both company-related and passenger communications. In other parts of the world, such as the Far East, Europe, and the Pacific region, a similar datalink system called SITA-Aircom is in use. SITA (Société Internationale de Telecommunications Aeronautiques) is planning on expanding its satellite-linked Aircom service. Japan also has its own datalink capability called JAL/NTT, and Air Canada handles datalink capability for Canada.

7.3. Transponder Datalink Communication

A study by professional operators, reported by Fellman and Lucier (1989, 15), concludes "that approximately 80 percent of ATC system errors are caused by inadequate voice communication, usually between pilot and controller." To reduce these errors and to make communications more efficient, standardized-format air-ground information can be transmitted in a digital form via a datalink, such as the Class 3 or Class 4 Mode S transponder.

The Mode S transponder responds to ATC-initiated position and altitude interrogations and also serves as an information datalink between the aircraft and ATC. The FAA's AERA plan (see section 2.2) indicates that the Mode S transponder will serve to receive digitally data-linked clearances, sector handoffs, special-use airspace advisories, and weather information (such as current and forecast weather, winds-aloft reports, and even ATIS information) from ATC. Similarly, for aircraft suitably equipped with some form of centralized avionics system or dedicated crew-interface equipment, the pilot can initiate a clearance request in a standardized format to ATC via Mode S. The automated ATC system will receive this request, analyze it with respect to the total ATC traffic situation, and respond appropriately to the aircraft via Mode S, all automatically with a minimum of human workload and using no voice communication at all. Once the clearance is received in this form, the centralized avionics system can, with pilot approval, distribute the revised clearance information to appropriate subsystems. For example, a revised altitude or heading would be provided to the autopilot's mode control panel (MCP), a revised altimeter setting would be provided to the air data system, a route change would be provided to the flight management system, a frequency change would be provided to the radio tuning panel, etc. If weather information is uplinked, the onboard system can enter the weather data into its own databank, the electronic library system, for example. The point is that in the future this kind of communication can be handled via digital datalink rather than by voice transmission.

The military uses a similar menu-driven, preformatted datalink capability in tactical battle situations. The system prompts the pilot to select the desired message parameters from menu lists. Since the message information types are preformatted, the desired message can be specified quickly and then transmitted by a digital datalink burst to a preselected receiver. Likewise, since most air traffic messages can be standardized — a request for altitude change, revised routing, weather data — the pilot can build a message from a menu selection and then send it via the Mode S datalink to ATC. By the same token, ATC can datalink most handoffs, clearance revisions, advisories, etc., via digital datalink burst. The advantages of preformatted datalink communications are clear: they reduce the possibility of misinterpretation and poor reception (thus ensuring higher communication reliability), and they increase transmission speed (thus reducing frequency congestion).

Obviously, datalink communication requires additional equipment that not all aircraft will have, in which case voice communication will still be used. Voice communication will also continue to be used to a large extent in terminal areas to facilitate takeoff and landing clearances without requiring the pilot to focus attention on formatting a datalink message. In high-density terminal areas, dynamic com capability favors voice even with its added on-frequency congestion. This is because voice communications contribute to heightened pilot awareness of the traffic situation. As the tempo of voice communications picks up, pilots tend to increase their vigilance and mentally tune in more to terminal area activity. This has often been referred to as the party-line effect, where the listeners gain valuable situation awareness.

The Mode S datalink capability is also used in conjunction with collision-avoidance equipment. This form of datalink communication automatically coordinates conflict resolution and escape maneuvers between two aircraft that are TCAS-equipped (see section 7.6).

The Mode S transponder is an improvement over its predecessors, all ATCRBS (air traffic control radar beacon system) transponders. It reduces false aircraft tracks for ATC radar surveillance, reduces synchronous garble existing with previous transponders, and allows aircraft to be identified and tracked individually with fewer interrogations. Because of Mode S transponders, the future ATC system (described in section 2.2) will function more effectively and provide more services.

The 1990s is the decade for implementation of the first operational Mode S ground sensors that permit two-way datalink capability. Datalinked weather service includes pilot reports, radar summary reports, surface observations, winds-aloft forecasts, terminal forecasts, and hazardous weather advisories. Some Mode S datalinked ATC messages may be possible by 1993. These messages include sector handoffs, altitude assignments, enroute minimum-safe-altitude warnings, and ATIS (automatic terminal information service) data. After this initial set of services, predeparture clearance delivery and NOTAMs will be implemented. Scheduled for 1994 are uplink reports of traffic, route forecasts, hazardous weather graphic maps, airspace advisories, and runway surface winds. Downlink reports will include pilot reports. In the military arena, datalink capability will allow coordination of multiple aircraft and sharing of sensor and tactical information, thus optimizing both offensive and defensive combat effectiveness.

Most new transponder installations for aircraft must be Mode S after January 1, 1992. Existing transponders do not have to be replaced with Mode S, however. For many years to come, then, there will continue to be a mix of Mode S transponders and older transponders with no datalink capability. The FAA estimates that even by the year 2000 only about 32 percent of the aircraft in the United States will be Mode S-equipped. The rest of the world may lag behind indefinitely.

Special Committee 142 of the Radio Technical Commission for Aeronautics (RTCA) controls the Mode S performance standards. The committee has required all transponder manufacturers to comply with the open systems interconnection (OSI) standard so that future datalink systems will be compatible with Mode S.

7.4. Satellite Communication (Satcom)

The use of satellites as a means to communicate is not new. On October 4, 1957, the Soviet Union launched the first satellite, spurring NASA to launch its first communication satellite in 1958. Transoceanic satellite telephone transmissions and maritime satcom capability are well established now, to say nothing of the extensive use of satellites for television transmissions. The first successful aviation satcom test was conducted in 1964. General satcom capability did not develop quickly, however, because the need was not immediate and the funding was not forthcoming. By the late 1980s the desire for better transoceanic communications capability served as a catalyst for satcom. It is the most feasible and reliable means to serve large numbers of users over wide coverage areas with high quality. In addition satellite links promise to handle huge amounts of data, satisfying the communication needs of a large number of users. Aviation satcom capability is currently in an intermediate stage of planning, development, and phase-in.

Since the launch of Telstar-1 in 1962, airlines have wanted to use satellite communication over the oceans because of the poor signal-propagation characteristics of HF systems. The need for improved air-ground ATC communication is not the only catalyst to push satcom into being. The need of the airlines for better operational communication and the entrepreneurial thrust to provide commercial telephone service for airline passengers are also driving satcom advances. Passenger telephone service is of particular interest because it could attract business passengers and increase revenues. Skyphone, a consortium of companies in the United Kingdom, Norway, and Singapore, initiated the world's first aeronautical satellite telephone service with a six-month trial in 1989 on a British Airways flight from London to New York. This telephone service will evolve into other related services, such as FAX capability.

The developing satcom service will satisfy four aviation needs:

1. Air traffic control communications, including ATS (air traffic services) messages
2. Airline company communications, such as dispatch and operational information, onboard inventories, weather data, etc. — basically the ACARS information that is often called AOC (airline operational communications)
3. Passenger telephone service, including APC (aeronautical passenger communications)
4. Automatic dependent surveillance (ADS), which involves transmitting aircraft positions back to ATC automatically so ATC can derive a pseudo-radar display of aircraft positions

ADS was conceived by the FAA in January 1985 and is being further developed by the FAA. It involves automatic position and altitude reports from aircraft to ATC via a satellite datalink. It is a good application for satcom because it requires only narrow bandwidths and, therefore, does not impose much load on satellite channels. ADS will be valuable for flights over oceans, deserts, jungles, remote areas, and mountainous terrain, and for flights at low altitudes, where aircraft are often not within the line-of-sight requirement for standard VHF voicecom systems. Currently, for example, over oceans the normal VHF voice-com link between aircraft and ATC does not suffice because of the short-range line-of-sight limitation of VHF radio. Airliners must rely on long-range HF voice communication, which is hindered by propagation effects.

Because of the problems of current long-range oceanic communications and because only infrequent (hourly or every 10 degrees of longitude) position reports are transmitted, transoceanic flights are spaced with excessive separation (2,000 feet vertically, 10 minutes or 60 miles in trail). This helps to ensure safety in the event of communication interruption. Transoceanic aircraft are routed along fixed oceanic lanes and generally do not have much freedom to choose fuel-efficient direct routes. The use of reliable satellite communication can make smaller separation standards possible (e.g., 1,000 feet vertically, 5 minutes or 10 miles in trail) and therefore meet increased traffic-flow densities.

The FAA's ADS program was organized into two steps. The functional specification for Step 1 was completed in January 1988 and involved a demo program for one-way downlink of position and altitude reports every five minutes via automatic satellite transmissions. ATC uplink communications in this phase still used HF. The Step 1 operational readiness demonstration began in early 1990. Step 2 involves two-way pilot-controller satcom capability with a demonstration sometime in 1993. Once initial ADS capability is established by mid-1995, other capability will be added, such as two-way free-text messages, preformatted clearance and request messages, and digital voice.

Currently, multiple satcom ventures are emerging to serve the aviation market. Inmarsat (International Maritime Satellite Organization) was established in 1979 as a forty-eight-nation consortium to provide maritime users with satcom capability. At first it operated only in a maritime frequency band adjacent to the aeronautical satellite band, but its spectrum was underutilized by maritime users. So Inmarsat voted in 1985 to expand business to include the aeronautical market.

In 1989, after a series of FCC hearings, a company called Comsat was granted rights to provide satellite communications in the United States using the Inmarsat system. Another company called AMSC (American Mobile Satellite Corporation) was also granted rights to offer satcom access to providers of satcom capability. Initially AMSC will probably use the Inmarsat system obtained through Comsat and will provide air traffic communications as well as passenger communication services. Probably by the end of 1994, AMSC will have its own satellite system and will offer voice communication service.

Inmarsat's third-generation satellites, all called Inmarsat-3, are scheduled for deployment in the mid-1990s and will provide oceanic air route coverage with eight times the channel capacity of the previous-generation satellites. Since Inmarsat already has satellites and ground stations in place to serve the maritime market, it has the best potential to make some form of cost-effective low-risk international satellite communication possible for the aviation market. It demonstrated two-way satellite datalink capability in 1985 and is working closely with ICAO-FANS (future air navigation systems committee) and ARINC-AEEC (Airline Electronic Engineering Committee) to establish standard characteristics and protocols for satellite communications. It provides free use of its satcom system for experimental and demonstration purposes.

Another satellite venture is AvSat (Aviation Satellite Corporation), a subsidiary of ARINC (Aeronautical Radio, Inc.), the airline-owned communications company. AvSat, incorporated in March 1986 and controlled by the airlines, realized early the need for improved worldwide communication capability, not only for airline company communication but also for ATC communication and other purposes, such as passenger telephone service. AvSat had planned to initiate satcom capability over the continental United States and then expand the coverage to include oceanic regions. However, in 1989 the FCC denied ARINC's application to provide U.S. satcom service. ARINC is still planning to provide international satcom service, probably in cooperation with SITA (Société Internationale de Telecommunications Aeronautiques). SITA was founded in 1949 and currently serves 314 member airlines worldwide. It operates in 170 countries and has the world's largest specialized telecommunications network. Currently, Northwest, United, British Airways, Quantas, Japan Air Lines, American, Air France, KLM, and other airlines are including satcom capability onboard some of their new aircraft.

Early system testing included medium-speed data transmissions (600 bits per second) of airline operational information, weather, position reporting, and ATC messages. Future data rates will likely increase as much as tenfold over the next twenty years. Eventually, voice transmissions will be digitized, primarily for ATC communication. Much work is also being done in the area of aircraft antenna design to develop high-gain, low-profile antennas that will contribute to better satcom capability.

The FANS working group of ICAO and the AEEC subgroup of ARINC are developing specifications for system characteristics that should ensure international standards and equipment compatibility. The idea of open systems interconnection (OSI) is being advanced, which would require equipment to be designed for compatibility with other interoperable equipment and systems.

The major factors affecting aeronautical use of satellites, at least until the mid-1990s, will involve aircraft antenna development and a push to reduce cost per channel. No doubt satellites developed for aviation use will have boosted power to permit smaller aircraft antennas. Likewise, satellite receiver sensitivity should increase to reduce the power output requirement for aircraft terminals. The number of satellite channels available will increase to reduce the user cost per channel. The future AMSC satellite system is expected, for example, to accommodate as many as four thousand simultaneous voice channels.

In the long run, high-efficiency modulation and coding schemes will permit increased channel capacity and lower cost per channel. Satcom benefits will include more reliable long-range communication capability for all altitudes, remote areas, and offshore areas; high-quality data and voice communication, including passenger telephone, FAX, and Telex services; data transmission to and from ATC for clearance changes, weather, position reports, etc.; and aircraft operational data transmission to company dispatch centers, including engine and fuel data, system status, out/off/on/in times, and other maintenance data. With the availability of reliable and accurate ADS aircraft position and altitude information, air safety will be enhanced and aircraft operating costs will be reduced as aircraft fly optimum flight tracks.

I should reemphasize, however, that while satcom fills a real need in transoceanic communicating, it is likely that most continental and terminal-area communications will continue to be dominated by VHF radio for the foreseeable future. Nevertheless, it is still likely that a datalink such as Mode S will become an integral part of VHF communication.

7.5. Aeronautical Telecommunication Network

The ACARS datalink, SITA-Aircom, and other datalink services are currently heavily used. The character-oriented ACARS is being phased out in favor of the bit-oriented AVPAC datalink. Other datalinks, such as satcom and the Mode S datalink, will be available by the mid-1990s. Realizing the potential problems of this proliferation of different datalink systems, the FAA commissioned MITRE Corporation to invent an organized telecommunication scheme. The result is ATN (aeronautical telecommunication network), as shown in figure 7.1.

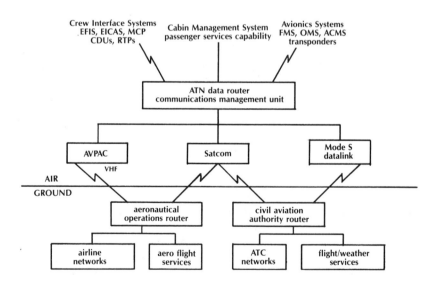

Figure 7.1. Aeronautical telecommunication network

ATN is a global, aeronautical, digital data network architecture that facilitates data transfer between multiple onboard avionics systems and multiple ground telecommunication networks using a common addressing scheme, common OSI protocol, and multiple data-distribution methods. The onboard systems include crew-interface systems, a cabin management system (including passenger communication services,) as well as other avionics systems. The ground networks include the ATC system, airline company systems, and other public (and even private) systems. The data-distribution methods include AVPAC, the Mode S datalink, and satcom. The ATN network structure will result in better message-transfer reliability. ATN will also contribute to better ATC flight handling and improved onboard information availability, such as real-time weather data.

The nodes in the various networks are individually addressable to permit end-to-end data routing. OSI is a protocol framework that facilitates interoperability with the industry-wide telecommunication infrastructure. ATN will select the optimal data-distribution datalink automatically. An onboard ATN data router will select the AVPAC, satcom, or Mode S datalink, as appropriate, for efficient data transmission. This router will also distribute incoming messages to the appropriate onboard system. On the ground, routers will distribute downlinked data to the appropriate network and addressee.

The Radio Technical Commission for Aeronautics (RTCA) is responsible for preparing the ATN minimum operational standards (MOPS), and ICAO is also developing international ATN standards.

7.6. Collision-alerting Communication

Collision-alerting equipment requires a form of automatic communication between aircraft via onboard transponders. All pilots know that when they are in visual meterological conditions (VMC) they are ultimately responsible for collision avoidance and must rely on the see-and-avoid principle. When they are in instrument meteorological conditions (IMC) and under ATC control, this responsibility rests with ATC. While the responsibility for maintaining collision avoidance is clearly defined, in practice this scheme is not foolproof. In VMC, for example, situations may develop that take the pilot's eyes away from looking for traffic; or the weather conditions, while officially VMC, may still be hazy; or another aircraft may be in a pilot's blindspot, such as below and ahead on descent. In IMC there is no guarantee that keeps violators (non-IFR traffic) out of the weather; an IFR flight descending in the clouds may break out just under the clouds and collide with VFR traffic.

ATC and pilots alike try their utmost for their own sakes to prevent inflight collisions, but on rare occasions aircraft converge. Only about 2 percent of all aircraft accidents are the result of midair collisions. In fact, between 1938 and 1986, of 1,868 air-carrier accidents only fifty were midairs (Lacagnina 1986, 61). Nevertheless, the press coverage given to each aircraft accident has heightened public concern. As a result, the FAA has pushed for the use of collision-alerting equipment on airliners, even though the cost is high.

A major thrust for collision-avoidance systems started in 1956 after a DC-7 and a Super Constellation collided high over the Grand Canyon in VMC weather. Only a year earlier, RTCA, the Air Transport Association (ATA), and the predecessor of the Institute for Electrical and Electronics Engineers (IEEE), in a joint statement, had urged industry to develop a collision-alerting system called ACAS (airborne collision-avoidance system). ACAS was initially a noncooperative, radar-based system that depended on technology that was not yet mature. By 1960 it was clear that a cooperative technique was needed so aircraft could communicate some kind of relative position information. Other ACAS testing continued into the 1970s, but the major problem was that too many phantom (i.e., false) targets were detected.

Under pressure from Congress in 1974, the FAA took an initiative that involved the onboard transponder and the ATC radar beacon system. The new concept was called BCAS (beacon collision-avoidance system), but BCAS failed to handle adequately the numerous targets in high-density areas. A separate ground-based system called ATARS (automatic traffic-advisory and resolution service) was conceived to handle collision avoidance in dense terminal areas. Meanwhile, the search to solve the BCAS problems led to early Mode S transponder concepts. On June 23, 1981, the current TCAS (traffic-alert and collision-avoidance system) concept was born as a modification to BCAS. It uses different interrogation techniques to reduce garble and frequency saturation.

As discussed in section 2.2, the ATC system is striving to improve its collision-avoidance capability, and this capability will continue to get better for aircraft under ATC control. In addition to improving ground-based collision-avoidance capability, onboard TCAS equipment is intended to alert pilots that other aircraft are in close proximity and to suggest a means of escape. The safety advantages are obvious. Another benefit may be the eventual reduction of separation for TCAS-equipped aircraft to expedite traffic flow and increase airport arrival capacity. As an initial step in this direction, transoceanic flight separation could be reduced from sixty to ten miles. TCAS may even permit closer arrival separation and use of parallel runways to alleviate arrival congestion.

The simplest form of TCAS, called TCAS 1, provides proximity traffic advisories only, not resolution recommendations, and is intended for general aviation and small commercial aircraft use. TCAS 1 development has been somewhat dormant in favor of TCAS 2 development. However, at least one version of TCAS 1 is being developed as a relatively low-cost passive system; that is, it does not transmit any interrogations. This system listens to other transponders that are responding to ATCRBS interrogations and computes their position (within 5 degrees azimuth), velocity, relative altitude, and track.

TCAS 2 is currently in the deployment stage. It detects potential conflicting traffic within approximately 15 nm ahead and 7.5 nm behind with an accuracy of 9 degrees, and it provides vertical escape recommendations to the pilot. Actually, the dimensions of the collision-detection airspace are based on closure rates (up to 1,200 knots horizontally and 10,000 feet vertically) and geometries as well as on variable signal sensitivity levels; therefore, they cannot be expressed exactly by distance. TCAS 2 can handle traffic densities of at least twenty-four aircraft within 5 nm.

An advanced version of TCAS called TCAS 3 is in development. TCAS 3 has a directional accuracy of 2 degrees and provides horizontal as well as vertical conflict-resolution recommendations. Table 7.1 summarizes the capability provided by the onboard TCAS system. For the system to be effective, both aircraft must be TCAS-equipped.

TCAS 2 and TCAS 3 are used with a Mode S transponder that interrogates other transponders on nearby aircraft and tracks their range and altitude. The maximum capability is achieved when the intruder aircraft also has a Mode S transponder. Then conflict-resolution maneuvers are coordinated via datalink between the two aircraft involved

Table 7.1. Capability of onboard TCAS

| Onboard System | Transponder Capability of Other Aircraft | | |
	Mode A	Mode C/S	TCAS 2/3
TCAS 1	proximity	proximity	proximity
TCAS 2	proximity	proximity	proximity
		V resolution	V resolution
			coordination
TCAS 3	proximity	proximity	proximity
		V/H resolution	V/H resolution
			coordination

Proximity: Onboard system detects nearby aircraft.

V resolution: Onboard system provides vertical escape resolution.

V/H resolution: Onboard system provides vertical escape or horizontal escape resolution.

Coordination: Onboard system coordinates escape resolution with systems of other aircraft.

to prevent mirror-image escape commands. The Mode S transponder is controlled by TCAS to vary its output power level (called "whisper-shout" capability) during TCAS interrogations. This power level is also controllable by ATC to prevent TCAS interrogations from saturating ATC interrogations in high-density terminal areas.

Some aircraft are equipped with Mode C transponders, which do not provide full Mode S capability but do encode aircraft altitude into the output signal. If the intruder aircraft is equipped with a Mode C transponder, TCAS can still give a vertical escape recommendation. If the intruder is not at least Mode C–equipped, TCAS can detect potential threats but cannot provide an escape recommendation.

The onboard TCAS equipment, then, depends on equipping all other aircraft with transponders to facilitate the detection of proximity or closure conditions. The FAA's long-range push is to get all aircraft equipped with at least the Mode C transponders. Currently, Mode C is required in the following cases as of the dates indicated:

1. At and above 10,000 MSL (July 1, 1989)
2. Within 30 nm of all TCAs, surface to 10,000 MSL (July 1, 1989)
3. Within all airport radar service areas (December 30, 1990)
4. Within 10 nm radius of designated airports (December 30, 1990)

With multiple and independent systems, including pilots' visual checking, ATC collision-detection capability, and onboard TCAS capability, the chance of midair collisions will be reduced significantly. Based on a scale of 1.0 without TCAS, the FAA estimates that with TCAS the risk of a midair collision is reduced to 0.25. With the new Mode C transponder requirements for aircraft in effect, the risk would be reduced further to 0.123 (Tippins 1988b, 64).

A prototype TCAS 2 that began initial evaluation in 1982 was certified in 1986 for operational evaluation. The FAA started a flight-test program for TCAS in February 1986. The first production TCAS 2 units received FAA equipment acceptance in 1990. The FAA's current requirement, dictated by legislation passed in December 1987, is for all commercial aircraft with more than thirty seats to be equipped with TCAS 2 by the end of 1993. Commuter and air-taxi aircraft with from ten to thirty seats probably will be required to have TCAS 1 by February 1995.

Unfortunately, TCAS will not be the universal solution to midair collisions, even in conjunction with continuing improvements in ATC capability to look ahead and plan for aircraft separation, because TCAS equipment is currently projected to be far too costly for installation in anything but airliners and upper-level corporate and commercial aircraft. The hope is that eventually TCAS prices may come down enough to be considered for many general aviation aircraft. In the meantime, TCAS-equipped aircraft will provide significant safety advantages for the everyday airline passenger. The problem of midairs and near-misses with nonequipped aircraft will have to await a more cost-effective solution.

Additional information, such as the intruder aircraft's type and airspeed, may eventually be included in TCAS displays to facilitate visual identification of the traffic and the appropriate escape maneuver. In the longer term, it is possible that the TCAS function may be incorporated into the highly integrated, centralized system-management avionics equipment discussed in chapter 4. Then the central system can correlate other sensory information and aircraft situation parameters to automatically, upon pilot command, respond to a conflict alert and fly an optimized resolution maneuver.

7.7. Summary

Communicating via digital datalink will help solve many problems associated with voice communication by handling routine coordination transmissions, such as simple requests and acknowledgments, as well as for more complex clearances and weather reports. The new Mode S transponder with datalink capability will be used in the future as an ATC datalink. More use will also be made of the existing ACARS (or a similar) datalink system to convey airline operational messages. Datalink capability typically improves communication accuracy, but at the same time it can add to crew workload. While datalink has many advantages, voice still offers dynamic communication flexibility. Datalink communication has ramifications for message interpretation, understanding, and use that are, as yet, not clearly understood.

Future communication will also involve satellite-based repeaters to solve communication problems during flights over oceans, deserts, jungles, or mountains. Satcom will serve the needs for ATC communication, airline company communication, passenger telephone service, and automatic dependent surveillance (ADS), in which aircraft will datalink their positions to ATC when direct radar surveillance is unavailable.

Another form of communication capability is the TCAS collision-avoidance system, which involves the automatic transponder communication of aircraft proximity between equipped aircraft. This onboard collision-avoidance capability will complement the separation service currently provided by ATC and will provide onboard separation assurance. Although the midair collision rate for aircraft is very low, the goal is to prevent all midairs. TCAS capability is a move in this direction.

8. Flight Control Advances

8.1. Introduction

The Wright brothers in 1903 used wing warping (twisting the wing) to control their airplane's banking. Aircraft designers soon found that banking could be accomplished more easily by using hinged trailing-edge wing ailerons that deflected oppositely on each side. These ailerons, and also the other aerodynamic surfaces (elevator, rudder, flaps, tabs, slats, etc.), were connected with cables to the pilot's cockpit controls. Later, mechanical pushrods became popular. By the late 1940s, as aircraft became larger in size, the control surfaces and aerodynamic forces were larger, and the interconnecting cables and pushrods became heftier. Eventually, the controls became so heavy and required so much pilot strength that hydraulic boosting was used to ease the control pressures. Functional availability concerns led to dual, triple, and even quadruple redundancy of hydraulic, servo, and actuation systems and to the attendant added weight and complexity.

As electronics became more sophisticated and reliable, the concept of electronically controlled flight surfaces was introduced. Called fly-by-wire (FBW), this concept involves electronic sensing of the pilot's control inputs and electronic transmission of signals via wires to servos at each flight control aerodynamic surface to actuate those surfaces. Fly-by-wire capability eliminates the weight of the mechanical connections between the pilot's controls and the flight control surfaces. Ken Thompson (1988, 20) detailed the benefits of electric actuators: improved maintainability, reduced logistics, better redundancy management, greater reliability, and in most cases reduced life-cycle costs. This chapter deals with FBW advanatges and other electronic advances in the area of flight control.

144

8.2. Fly-by-Wire

In a typical fly-by-wire flight control system, FBW computers receive the signals from the pilot's controls and then electronically drive the actuators. An electrical "back-drive" system is used to apply forces to the pilot's controls. This gives the pilot artificial tactile feel of the controls. The FBW system analyzes and manipulates the signals with the following benefits:

It can detect and prevent the pilot from overcontrolling the aircraft and exceeding airspeed and aerodynamic envelope limits (stalls, load factors, pitch and roll attitudes).
It can perform stability augmentation functions because it has control of individual aerodynamic surfaces.
It can alleviate maneuvering and wind-gust loads.
It can permit relaxed static stability and improved aerodynamic efficiency.

A number of other benefits are commonly attributed to FBW:

Automatic precision trimming
Multiple redundancy
Better maneuverability; i.e., more stability, precision, and flexibility
Lower production and maintenance costs
Lower weight (The Airbus A320 system weighs 771 pounds *less* than a mechanical system, for example.)

As an example of the benefits of FBW, consider straight-and-level flight in mild turbulence. The FBW system has aircraft attitude information from gyro or inertial systems as well as multiaxis accelerations and air data (e.g., vertical and horizontal pressure changes). When turbulence causes a change in the aircraft's attitude, the FBW system can control the appropriate aerodynamic surfaces to compensate for the attitude change and to alleviate gust loads. Likewise, FBW technology holds promise as an effective means to maintain flight control when pilots encounter windshear, with its localized, abrupt, and violent wind changes.

FBW technology dates back to the early space program, in which digital control was used to fire spacecraft attitude thrusters. Engineers at NASA's Dryden Flight Research Center contemplated digital flight control for aircraft as early as 1968. NASA claims the first success in employing full-authority digital FBW technology. In the early 1970s they converted a space program FBW system for a Vought F-8 Crusader. This development effort was later carried over to the space shuttle FBW control system.

Early FBW capability began with feedback stabilization. Airplane stability was monitored with air data and motion sensors. These data were fed back to the primary flight control system, which still involved conventional mechanical linkages and actuators. Additional small-authority stabilization aerodynamic FBW systems were added for stability augmentation to damp pitch, roll, and yaw oscillations.

As with the introduction of most new technologies, developers took a cautious approach with fly-by-wire. For example, although analog FBW has been used in the Concorde since 1969, a mechanical backup system is also used. To gain experience with FBW capability, the Boeing 767 spoilers use FBW signals to the hydraulic actuators. The L-1011 also uses electrically controlled spoilers. The Airbus A310 (since 1983) and A300-600 (since 1984) use digital FBW for slats, flaps, and upper-wing surface devices only. The A320, which first flew February 22, 1987, was the first commercial transport to use FBW without mechanical backup except for pitch trim and rudder.

In the military arena (Rawles 1988, 42), the F-16 was "the first production fighter aircraft ever to have had its mechanical stick and rudder controls replaced with digital controls." The F-117A stealth fighter, which first flew in June 1981, owes its ability to fly despite a very unusual shape to its FBW flight control system. One of today's most advanced examples of the application is the Grumman X-29 fighter, which first flew in December 1984. The X-29 was intentionally designed with reduced inherent aerodynamic stability to take advantage of the resulting reduced drag and increased maneuverability. As a result of reduced stability, however, the X-29 must use a full-authority FBW digital flight control system (DFCS). All of the pilot's control inputs are sensed electronically, and the triple-redundant DFCS sends commands to the control surface actuators forty times a second. The triplex flight control computers constantly vote on their command outputs. If one computer fails, the other two outvote it, and the bad signal is ignored. If two computers fail, an emergency analog backup system takes over.

A major advantage of the FBW flight control system is that it permits more efficient aircraft aerodynamics for better maneuverability and better range and endurance performance. That is, an aircraft designed with inherently less stable aerodynamics can be smaller, lighter, and more maneuverable. Artificial stability is provided by the FBW system. Developers of the X-29 indicate that because of the nature of its flight control surfaces and FBW capability, this aircraft can withstand major damage to the flight control system, and the remaining aerodynamic surfaces can still be reconfigured for stable flight. The FBW system permits highly integrated interaxis coordination under varying axis-control situations. Regarding system availability, "the X-29's designers claim that the chances of a total system failure are lower than those with conventional mechanical control systems" (Rawles 1988, 43).

Fly-by-wire and fly-by-light flight control systems are trends for future sophisticated aircraft. The air force's advanced tactical fighter (section 3.2) will probably make use of digitally controlled aerodynamic contol surfaces as well as thrust vectoring.

8.3. Flight-by-Light (Fiber Optics)

Fly-by-light, which uses optical-fiber signal paths as opposed to wires, is a natural derivative of FBW and has the following advantages:

High data bandwidth for greater data-handling capability
Reduced size and weight
Virtually immune to electromagnetic interference (EMI) and electromagnetic pulse (EMP) radiation
No electrical fire hazard
May be used to advantage in composite aircraft that do not have metallic shielded skins

This fiber-optics technology was first used in aircraft in a flight test of a marine corps AV-8B in 1981, but it was used for data handling, not for flight control. On March 24, 1982, fiber-optics technology was demonstrated for the first time in the flight control system of an A-7D.

FBW and FBL flight control are especially valuable for helicopters, which are inherently unstable. In November 1981, the army contracted with Boeing Helicopter to develop the advanced digital optical control system (ADOCS) using a converted UH-60A helicopter as a testbed. The program used FBL flight control and a sidestick controller. On November 7, 1985, the helicopter flew for the first time as the "world's first optically linked, fully computerized flight-control system to fly" (Green 1988, 39). The system stabilizes the aircraft and permits the pilot to focus attention on navigational or mission tasks. The stability also makes nap-of-the-earth flight far easier than before. The army plans to apply this technology to its RAH (formerly LHX) light helicopter program (Green 1988, 39). According to project officer Maj. Gary Jerauld, FBL fiber optics is "the wave of the future, replacing standard electrical systems the way VHS is replacing Beta or the disk player is replacing records" (see Nelms 1988, 21). Besides its use in the RAH program, fiber-optics technology is also expected to be considered for the air force's ATF and NASA's X-30 NASP (see section 3.2).

There are also some negative aspects to fiber optics. According to John Rhea (1988, 103), they include "high costs, specialized training for repair and maintenance, low tensile strength of the fibers, and potential signal losses, particularly at the connectors."

Because one of the major benefits of fiber-optics buses is their high data-transmission capability, this technology will likely be used for applications like digital-map data transmission, rather than for flight control, especially since flight control is classified by the FAA as a critical function and therefore typically uses well-established and proven technologies.

8.4. Sidestick Controller

A sidestick controller is a hand-held, wrist-action control stick mounted on the side of the cockpit, as opposed to a stick or wheel column mounted between the pilot's legs. One advantage of a sidestick controller is that it does not obstruct the pilot's view of the instrument panel. Also, it is comfortable for the pilot to use. The pilot can rest the controlling arm on an armrest and grip the sidestick controller. Wrist action alone can move the sidestick forward, back, and sideways. This is particularly beneficial for tight fighter cockpits and high-G maneuvering, but the same control works just as well in transport aircraft. Most pilots believe that wrist-action sidestick controllers offer more precise control.

Sidestick controller research began in the mid-1950s, although sidesticks did not become viable until the advent of FBW technology. They have a digital interface, rather than a mechanical interface, with the flight control system. The FBW flight control computers sense control movement from the pilot's wrist action, and then they drive the aerodynamic surfaces via electronic signals. The FBW computers may intervene, if they are so configured, to prevent the pilot from overcontrolling the aircraft to the point of stalling, overstressing the airframe, etc. Another advantage for the FBW sidestick controller is that the aircraft will remain in the attitude and flight path that it was in when the pilot's hand was removed. The Airbus A320 with sidestick controllers, for example, "even when left completely uncorrected by its pilots . . . will maintain an initially safe flight-path in response to an engine failure" (Baud 1988, 22).

For two-pilot crews, the FBW flight control computers sense both sidestick controller inputs and mix the two signals appropriately before driving the aerodynamic surfaces. The mixing logic can vary with the aircraft type and mission. One possibility is to blend each sidestick input with equal weighting, as is done in the A320. Another alternative is to give priority to the captain's control inputs. With the A320, either pilot may push a button on the controller to take control.

Another valuable function of a sidestick controller is its use (on the A320, for example,) in windshear recovery. The controller is simply pulled fully back. This automatically results in the autothrottle applying full go-around power and the FBW system configuring the aircraft for maximum lift.

Wrist-action controllers hold much promise for better aircraft control. The space shuttle has a wrist-action, four-axis hand controller for the mechanical arm that lifts payloads from the cargo bay. Grant McLaren (1988, 93) discusses the advantages for helicopters: "Today a four-axis single-hand controller has the potential to revolutionize helicopter cockpit design and control systems. It may replace both cyclic and collective controls of rotorwing aircraft with a single hand-operated guidance system. As a multi-dimensional computer-input device, the controller will be able to govern an aircraft in any axis in response to simple movements of one hand." This would alleviate helicopter-control workload tremendously.

8.5. Autoland Capability

The capability to land an airplane automatically has existed for some time. The first automatic landing with passengers on board happened in 1967 with a British European Airways Trident. By early 1989 more than 100,000 automatic landings had been completed with passengers on board (Sutton 1989, 315).

Automatic landing capability controlled by a coupled autopilot involves very complex control laws to transition the airplane from a stable approach descent to touchdown and then through the decelerating rollout. Typically, the flare, or touchdown transition, begins at about 50 feet as measured by the radio altimeter. The autopilot begins to raise the airplane nose using elevator actuators. At about the same time, the autothrottle begins to reduce engine power. At the point of touchdown, the aircraft has a pitch-high attitude to reduce the downward vertical speed to about 100 to 150 feet per minute, and the engine power has been reduced to idle. The coordination of pitch and power must be very precise so that touchdown occurs smoothly at the correct airspeed. Inertial rates and attitudes may also be used to help smooth the touchdown. After touchdown, full autorudder capability will control the airplane's rollout by keeping it centered on the localizer until the plane has slowed to taxi speed.

Various categories of autoland capability are defined as indicated in table 8.1. Note that each category has decision height (DH) and electronically determined runway visual range (RVR) visibility constraints. The values listed are the lowest these categories permit. For each category, there are requirements for aircraft equipment and certification, airport facilities and obstacles, and for pilot training and authorization. The actual operating limits depend on these other factors and may be higher than indicated in the table.

Table 8.1. Categories of autoland capability

Category	Decision Height (DH)	Visibility (RVR)
	feet	*feet*
1	200	1,800
2	100	1,200
3A[ab]	50	700
3B[cd]	50 > DH ≥ 0	150
3C[ca]	0	0

Sources: "Criteria for Approving Category I and Category II Landing Minima for FAR 121 Operators," *FAA Advisory Circular 120–29* (Sept. 25, 1970); "Criteria for Approval of Category III Landing Weather Minima," *FAA Advisory Circular 120–28C* (Mar. 9, 1984).

[a]Fail-passive autopilot required (i.e., autopilot failure disconnects autopilot without affecting flight path)

[b]Manually controlled touchdown required

[c]Fail-operational autopilot required (i.e., major component failure does not cause loss of functional capability)

[d]Automatic rollout guidance required

In 1989 there were thirty-three airports in Europe and nineteen in the United States equipped and certified for Category 3 operations (Sutton 1989, 315). Category 3 approaches can automatically take an airplane all the way to the ground. For Category 3B operations with zero DH, the RVR requirement exists because the autorollout is only fail-passive, while autoland must be fail-operational. Full autoland capability, which will land an airplane in zero ceiling and zero visibility conditions (called Category 3C autoland), is really a zero-zero taxi capability and is still unheard of because these weather conditions are so rare and certification for Category 3C has such stringent requirements.

Obviously the push to attain Category 3 autoland capability will depend on the need. In general, Europe is a long way ahead of the United States because of its higher population densities, greater competition from surface transport (roads/rail), smaller geographic area, and high incidence of radiation fog. Swissair, for example, has pushed very hard for Category 3 capability because of the weather in its service area. Category 3B operations will allow on-time flight schedules even in frequent poor-weather conditions. Swissair is the first airline to claim an all–Category 3 fleet, but British Airways probably has more Category 3 operations than any other airline. Regional operators in the sunny American southwest have much less need for Category 3 operations, and for them the benefits do not warrant the expense of this capability. The trend toward Category 3 autoland capability will likely continue to be selective and regional.

8.6. Windshear Avoidance and Recovery

Windshear is an abrupt change in wind direction and/or speed in a short time. Windshear below about one thousand feet above ground level can be critical to flight safety. At higher altitudes, abrupt wind changes are typically called clear-air turbulence and can still create severe problems for aircraft. However, at high altitudes aircraft are not so much in danger of crashing into the ground during recovery maneuvering.

Two airliner crashes—a July 1982 Pan American World Airways crash at New Orleans International Airport and an August 1985 Delta Airlines L-1011 crash at Dallas-Fort Worth International Airport—heightened the concern about windshear. Between 1965 and 1987, according to E. A. Murphy (1987, 11), windshear was a factor in thirty-two transport aircraft accidents, and more than six hundred fatalities were involved. Research begun in the 1980s and continuing in the 1990s focuses on the flight-critical problem of windshear and its predictive detection.

When windshear can be predicted (e.g., detected by Doppler radar) before the aircraft enters the windshear, then pilots can navigate around the hazardous activity. The latest generation of airborne weather radar systems may be able to detect microburst and windshear activity as much as ninety seconds in advance. If, however, windshear cannot be predicted but is detected only when encountered, then pilots must use reactive recovery maneuvers to escape from the windshear. Most of the available windshear-detection systems use the following inputs: accelerations, true airspeed, air temperature, pressure altitude, radio altitude, and pitch attitude or angle of attack. Their method is to detect inconsistencies between the atmospheric inputs and the aircraft flight-path momentum inputs in both the longitudinal and vertical axes.

After windshear is detected, some aircraft systems use flight-director pitch-guidance commands to help direct the pilot in the avoidance or recovery process. Currently, regulations require escape-guidance indications on all airline flight-director retrofit installations. Recovery has generally involved a maximum pitch attitude (just short of a stalling angle of attack) to avoid a descent, maximum engine thrust, and the existing flap and gear configuration. The idea is to use all of the aircraft's available energy to reduce the windshear-imposed descent rate. Other methods are also being analyzed for their effectiveness. Some aircraft systems, such as the MD-80 windshear detection and guidance system, permit autopilot and autothrottle coupling for automatic windshear recovery.

As an example, the Fokker 100 airliner has an autopilot-coupled windshear detection and escape function. It provides two levels of detection: (1) a red warning alert for decreasing aircraft performance when an unacceptable downdraft or severe tailwind is detected during a takeoff or approach, and (2) an amber caution alert for increasing aircraft performance when a headwind or an unusual updraft is detected during an approach. When a warning is generated, autopilot response is automatically initiated. During a takeoff, a windshear warning will cause automatic escape guidance. During an approach, a windshear warning will result in an automatic go-around escape sequence. The automatic escape guidance involves driving the thrust-management system to full power and driving the pitch system to maximum angle of attack.

Automating windshear recovery has an inherent problem—setting the initiation trigger. If the trigger is too sensitive, then nuisance operations will occur. If it is not sensitive enough, recovery will be unnecessarily delayed. What should be a warning system to avoid a hazardous situation becomes a recovery system that may not be adequate.

Researchers are investigating predictive windshear systems that use laser Doppler, microwave Doppler, and infrared techniques to detect emitted energy ahead of the aircraft. The infrared system senses the cooler microburst column of air as it shears vertically against the relatively warmer surrounding atmosphere. A pulsed laser-light technique holds promise for detecting clear-air turbulence ahead. Some predictive systems claim as much as a one-minute advance notice of low-level windshear and a several-minute notice of clear-air turbulence. Even a ten-second warning can be sufficient to permit engine spool-up and to begin pitch and power changes that may prevent a low-altitude disaster. Predictive systems can also detect the windshear effects associated with the jetstream and wingtip vortices.

By FAA directive, air carrier aircraft will be equipped with wind-shear-warning and flight-guidance systems by the mid-1990s. On September 22, 1988, the FAA issued a requirement for all airplanes with thirty or more seats to be equipped with a windshear-warning system by December 3, 1992. Later, this deadline was delayed a year to be concurrent with a proposed TCAS deadline of December 30, 1993.

Windshear-detection equipment is being located on the ground as well as in cockpits. On the ground, more than one hundred airports since 1978 have been equipped with low-level windshear-alerting systems (LLWAS), which use anemometers to detect microburst activity so that terminal area ATC facilities can warn aircraft in their areas. Also, as part of the terminal Doppler weather radar (TDWR) program, the FAA has installed forty-five Doppler radar systems at airports.

8.7. Other Flight Control Advances

In the future, thrust control may be integrated with sidestick-controller capability so that with one hand the pilot can control pitch, roll, and thrust. Thrust control would be achieved by fore-aft translation of the sidestick module.

Modern aircraft typically use a full-authority digital engine control (FADEC), which is FBW-like capability for the engines. A given power setting is selected by the pilot, and the FADEC translates this into optimum engine power over different flight conditions. This kind of electronic subsystem control is part of a general trend toward electronic flight control.

The air force's Aeronautical Systems Division (ASD) and NASA are involved in what is called the mission-adaptive wing program, which employs leading-edge and trailing-edge wing devices configured for changing conditions. A flexible composite-construction F-111 wing is fitted with 150 hydraulically powered actuators fed from the aircraft's FBW flight control system. The automated controls change the wing shape in order to produce the variable lift commanded by the pilot controls. An adaptive wing camber facilitates high maneuverability, supersonic speeds, and short-field takeoffs and landings.

In the future, aircraft force-bearing structural members may have sensors installed to measure real-time stress. Stress data could be used by the FBW flight control system to limit maneuvering loads on the aircraft. This may permit the use of lighter structures resulting in cost savings and improved performance. Maneuvering limits could prolong the life of an aircraft, especially if these limits are tightened as the airframe ages.

Other trends for the future indicate that system integration may consolidate the flight control system, the flight management system, and the propulsion system. This integrated consolidation will be more than just co-locating independent functions in the same box. For example, developers of the Grumman X-29 are planning on adding thrust vectoring to permit exceptional flight control in certain maneuvering regimes. The X-31 and F-22 ATF aircraft are also expected to use two-dimensional thrust vectoring. Additionally, for specialized military applications, the flight control system will likely become integrated with the weapons delivery system and the terrain-following and terrain-avoidance (TF/TA) system.

8.8. Summary

Fly-by-wire (FBW) flight control capability is one of the most significant advances being pursued in the flight control area. Although FBW has been used in military fighter aircraft for some time, it is still a relatively new capability for airliners. The advantages of FBW include lower weight, improved stability augmentation, better aerodynamic efficiency, and over control protection from pilot-induced stalls and from excessive load factors. In the future, the use of fiber-optic (fly-by-light or FBL) buses will be introduced because of their higher bandwidth and immunity to EMI/EMP. The electronic flight control capability that FBW and FBL provide has definite advantages for collision avoidance or windshear-escape maneuvering; when the pilot applies maximum deflection of the controls, the electronic flight control system will maneuver the aircraft up to the maximum safe limits without exceeding them.

Future aircraft may make more use of sidestick controllers to eliminate the control wheel, which obstructs the pilot's view of the instrument panel. Sidestick controllers will also permit a small table area in front of the pilot.

Automatic landing capability continues to be improved, but it is still not the trend for all landings. Autoland capability requires ground facilities for specific runways, and so autoland is typically used only on a regional basis when the weather requires it. In most regions the weather is not consistently bad, and operators will not accept the cost of equipping all of their aircraft with autoland capability. Some operators have a policy of requiring the use of autoland whenever it is available, while most use it only when needed. Nevertheless, Category 3 flight control capability is becoming standard for civil transport autopilots. For international operations especially, the disruption caused by even occasional diversions due to weather is unacceptable.

Improved windshear-detection systems are being developed. The emphasis is on predictive windshear-detection capability, which allows relatively mild avoidance maneuvering, rather than on reactive windshear-detection capability, which requires more severe maneuvering for escape.

9. Perspectives on the Future

9.1. Introduction

Avionics functional capabilities can be categorized from the perspective of how they support the flight crew's principal responsibilities of aviating, navigating, and communicating. Aviating involves controlling flight situation (i.e., precision control of aircraft attitude, altitude, airspeed, heading). Navigating involves controlling on-course movement from departure point to destination at an efficient rate while avoiding terrain, obstacles, and weather hazards. Communicating involves coordination between the flight crew and external elements, such as air traffic control, operations centers, and other aircraft (i.e., collision-avoidance communications); it also involves passenger communication services. Categorizing an avionics function from these perspectives helps to identify its role in relation to the flight crew's responsibility and its importance to the cockpit environment and flight situation awareness. Avionics advances are being made in all of these areas, and the trends for these advances are fairly clear.

9.2. Avionics Trends

Several constraints, limitations, and inadequacies are driving the need for avionics improvements today, notably:

Line-of-sight reception range for nav and com stations

Incomplete coverage areas, especially over oceans, mountains, and
  deserts
High-frequency (HF) propagation inconsistencies
Voice congestion
Limited frequency availability
Air traffic congestion, especially in terminal areas
Limited approach paths for terminal arrivals
Flight-route restrictions caused by ATC traffic-separation standards
Lack of onboard information about areas of real-time severe
  weather, turbulence, windshear, microburst activity, other at-
  mospheric conditions (e.g., winds or icing), nearby traffic, ter-
  rain, and obstacle elevations
Information overload in the cockpit
Control and display clutter
Aerodynamic inefficiency
Lack of avionics user-interface standardization
Mismatch between system functional capability and human per-
  formance capability

As a result, the capability and standards of nav and com systems are
evolving along with improvements in system design and functional capability. To address the navigation and communication deficiencies, a long-
range international vision is emerging that involves space-based satellite
nav (satnav) and satellite com (satcom) capability to provide continuous
global service.

Eventually satnav will be used as an approved sole-means-of-navigation capability and will make obsolete many of the systems we use
today for enroute, terminal, and approach guidance. Automatic dependent surveillance (ADS) will allow an aircraft to transmit its position
automatically (typically via satcom) to ATC, improving ATC surveillance in areas that lack primary radar coverage. This will increase safety
and will permit higher traffic-flow rates in these areas.

In terminal areas, highly precise and flexible microwave landing
systems (MLSs) are envisioned to permit straight-in, curved, or
segmented Category 2 and Category 3 approach paths with user-defin-
able glideslopes. This capability will support simultaneous approaches to
closely spaced (e.g., 2,500 feet of separation) parallel runways. MLS
might also be used for initial departure guidance.

It is possible that onboard satnav-based systems will synthesize a
virtual approach course and glideslope independent of any ground-based
guidance signals. This virtual approach path could be custom-tailored to
the performance characteristics of the specific aircraft and even to the
experience and proficiency levels of the pilot. Extending this concept one

step further, approaches could also be tailored to the dynamic traffic and weather conditions.

For landing guidance, improved high-integrity autoland capability will be available for landing under weather conditions of zero ceiling and zero visibility. Additionally, methods will evolve to permit better visual contact with the runway environment to allow the crew to control the flare and touchdown process manually. These methods will include improved infrared and millimeter-wave sensors for synthetic and enhanced vision as well as ground-based laser guidance techniques.

Once the aircraft is on the ground, high-speed runway turnoffs will allow reduced separation standards for approaches and increased flow rates for arrivals. Taxi-guidance navigation will also be available to facilitate low-visibility movement from runways to gates. Airport surface traffic control will have better surveillance capability for improved airport safety.

Satcom capability will include digital voice as well as datalink capability worldwide to improve operational communications as well as passenger communications. Satcom will be just one element of the aeronautical telecommunication network (ATN) that will also include the Mode S datalink associated with air traffic service and other private datalink services such as ACARS and AVPAC. These multiple com links will be coordinated using an onboard ATN router and a ground-based distribution router. ATN is envisioned as providing reliable, global, high-quality, wideband, digital communication capability between aircraft and ground telecommunication networks.

The onboard TCAS (traffic-alert and collision-avoidance system) is improving safety even as traffic densities increase. TCAS permits coordinated conflict detection and resolution autonomous from ATC separation service, and therefore it enhances collision avoidance. This may permit a reduction in the separation standards in the future, allowing higher traffic-flow rates.

Aircraft maneuverability, stability, aerodynamic efficiency, and overcontrol protection are improved by fly-by-wire (FBW) technology and its wideband counterpart, fly-by-light (FBL) technology. In the future, systems such as the TCAS, the ground-proximity warning system (GPWS), and windshear-avoidance capability may be coupled directly with the flight-envelope-protected FBW flight control system to improve flight safety.

Some clear trends are improving onboard avionics systems. They include

Aviating

Integration of flight control system (FCS), propulsion system, safety systems, and aerodynamic control systems

Introduction of energy management capability

Improved guidance-command display and enhanced vision capability

Fly-by-wire (FBW) and fly-by-light (FBL) fiber optics for aerodynamic efficiency and overcontrol protection

Stability augmentation for passenger comfort

Precision autoland capability for all-weather flight completion

Navigating

Transition to global navigation satellite systems (GNSS) with onboard automatic dependent surveillance (ADS) capability to support air traffic management

Precision 4D RNAV (area nav) accuracy in all flight phases (departure, enroute, and arrival)

Accommodation of preferred optimal flight profile (including route, altitude, and speed), even with dynamic weather and traffic conditions

Reduced separation standards and increased traffic-flow rates

Improved sensors to support nav and flight safety (e.g., Doppler radar, microwave and millimeter-wave radar, and infrared)

Predictive windshear and microburst detection, warning, and avoidance capability

Better terminal area navigational capability to facilitate arrival and departure sequencing and separation

Communicating

Transition to satellite-based communication (satcom), including digital voice and data capability

Faster and better communication capability through the use of digital datalink

Strategic communication capability, involving the aeronautical telecommunication network (ATN) and OSI-compatible ground communication networks

Improved strategic and tactical conflict avoidance, detection, and resolution

Additionally, advances in digital microelectronics involving very high processing throughput and extensive memory capacity, as well as improved high-resolution display capability with powerful graphics engines, are advancing many system-level trends. Over the decade of the 1990s, we will likely see the development of computers based on optical technology. These computers will employ laser-beam signals rather than electron flows. They will have processing speeds up to 100,000 times faster than speeds of conventional computers. These technical advances are fueling trends toward

Integrated but modular architectures for ease of growth

Open architecture, using industry standard parts, design, and interfaces (including the OSI model)

Fault-tolerant and robust system architectures with inherent graceful degradation involving redundant, reconfigurable modules and shared data resources

General-purpose, real-time, embedded, deterministic, multitasking processing capability

Advanced sensors with raw data processing at the sensor; data-intensive sensor fusion; imaging sensors with sophisticated image processing

Hardware and software partitioning for high integrity and better fault detection and isolation; good maintainability features

High reliability at the subsystem level and high functional availability at the system level

High-speed data-intensive distribution networks, including fiber-optic buses

Immunity to HIRF and EMI; environmentally stable and protected

Minimal size, weight, and power consumption

Past avionics advances have permitted the elimination of the radio operator, flight navigator, and the flight engineer positions in the cockpit. Future improvements should result in better avionics functional capability, integrity, and availability for the remaining crewmembers. At the operational level, systems will be optimized in

Larger flat-panel color displays with sharper resolution

Sophisticated, graphical, intuitive informational displays (including holographic imaging) for better situation awareness

Digital moving maps with real-time weather displays for superior navigation awareness

Improved user-interface methods (e.g., speech recognition and synthesis, cursor control, virtual control, touchscreen control, and spatial auditory cueing)

Common, multipurpose, centralized, standardized control and display capability

Better human-system integration and human-centered automation, resulting in improved workload management and operational simplicity

Better information access, management, and presentation

Use of artificial intelligence (AI) and expert systems (ES) capability to support flight crews and improve cockpit resource management and to improve human efficiency and effectiveness through situation evaluation and decision aiding

Future avionics will be more functionally useful and operationally simple. New avionics capability will emerge to help pilots manage information and to support better crew coordination and cockpit resource management. These avionics advances are especially valuable since today's flight crews are getting younger and new airplane systems are getting more sophisticated. Large panoramic displays with virtual 3D aspects will improve the crew's situation awareness. In the decade of the 1990s we are likely to see the introduction of pictorial displays of aircraft attitude and position instead of proliferating emulations of older electro-mechanical instruments.

In the past, avionics improvements have produced higher reliability and functional performance, but sometimes with the negative side-effects of higher acquisition costs, higher user workload, and higher maintenance complexity. Future emphasis will be placed on achieving cost-effective functionality, improved maintainability, and better human-system interfaces.

A combination of onboard nav and com avionics systems, their associated nav/com satellite infrastructures, and a modernized air traffic management system should result in the following benefits:

Accommodation of a wide mix of aircraft speeds and operating altitudes

Centralized ATC strategic management of traffic-flow planning and execution

Improved flow rates and higher airspace capacity with reduced traffic congestion

Semiautomatic ground-air (ATC-FMS) coordination and cooperation for more efficient user-preferred flight trajectories and departure-to-destination flight-path routing

Better onboard tactical flight planning

Better onboard conflict avoidance, detection, and resolution

Flight safety enhancements

9.3. Evolutionary Trends

The difference between an evolution and a revolution is largely one of expectation and timeframe. Evolution happens over time—in a natural, gradual, continuous progression. Revolution, on the other hand, is relatively fast-paced, unexpected, radical, fundamental change. The avionics trends described in this book, for the most part, are evolutionary. They are bound to happen; it is only a matter of time. Some advances, however, exhibit revolutionary characteristics. Satcom, satnav, and increased use of datalink communication were expected, but they involve a level of fundamental change. The transition from ground-based com and nav systems to space-based systems also involves fundamental change, as does the transition from voice communication to digital datalink.

Some would argue that fly-by-wire (FBW) capability is a revolutionary advance because it involves a radical, fundamental departure from the conventional aircraft control mechanisms. In this digital age, however, FBW capability was bound to happen, and it has existed for a long time in the military arena of highly agile advanced fighter jets. Moreover, it has taken many years for FBW to be transferred into the civil world of commercial avionics, so I maintain that FBW is primarily an evolutionary advance. Other system-level advances, such as integration, automation, information management, and graphics situation displays, are also evolutionary advances that are progressing as processing, memory, and other technological advances permit.

Likewise, advances such as the glass cockpit of CRT and flat-panel displays have had aspects of revolutionary change as well as of evolutionary expectations. Other innovative avionics concepts, such as TCAS, MLS, modular integrated avionics, and fiber-optics buses, exhibit both revolutionary and evolutionary characteristics. None of these advances has been particularly fast-paced or radical in nature. Therefore, the term *evolutionary* is a better primary descriptor. Safety-of-flight, transitional phase-in, and economic justification would also suggest an evolutionary dominance in avionics advances.

Although evolutionary in nature, the avionics advances in the decade of the 1990s should be very exciting and stimulating. The decade will very likely go down in history as a period in which previous avionics advances and trends converged and coalesced into highly integrated systems with synergistic and optimized functionality. In a sense, a *virtual revolution* is impending in the field of avionics in the major areas of communication, navigation, flight control, and system management.

In the decades leading up to the 1990s, advances in technology permitted significant improvements in existing avionics functionality and performance. Now new approaches to avionics functionality are emerging, such as higher levels of integration and human-centered automation, that provide better situation awareness through more intuitive informational displays and easier access to information.

Because of evolutionary constraints, avionics advances will progress as an orderly set of trends, rather than as disjointed, erratic advances on several fronts. A major reason for the orderliness is that some avionics functions, such as navigation and communication capability, are dependent on the established infrastructure of navaids and communication systems. This infrastructure has been ground-based, with networks of VOR stations, nondirectional beacons, LORAN chains, OMEGA sites, remote com relay stations, datalink relay strings, etc. In the 1990s we will see an evolutionary shift from ground-based infrastructures to a space-based complement of nav and com satellites. These satellite systems will provide much wider coverage with improved dependability and effectiveness.

At the same time, the new spaced-based infrastuctures will require even more multilateral international cooperation and mutual dependence than ever before. This is why, for example, ICAO established the Future Air Navigation Systems (FANS) committee on November 29, 1983. The FANS committee's charter includes making recommendations for international cooperation in the development of long-term communication, navigation, and surveillance (CNS) capability, projecting twenty-five years into the future. International cooperation is required to establish universal system standards as well as to gain worldwide acceptance of these systems. Multinational ownership and management of these systems will be necessary in order to ensure their acceptance.

One of the highest priorities that the FANS committee has identified is the worldwide global navigation satellite system (GNSS). GNSS will include GPS and probably the Russian GLONASS nav satellite system. Automatic dependent surveillance (ADS) is a key functional benefit of GNSS. ADS involves the transmission of onboard-determined positions to ATC in oceanic regions and other areas where ATC radar surveillance is lacking. This will permit better ATC management in these areas, resulting in reduced separation requirements and increased traffic-flow rates and safety.

In addition to the evolutionary advances already discussed, these evolutionary trends are continuing:

Transition from analog to digital electronics
Reduction in equipment size, weight, and power consumption

Passive cooling of equipment

Improvement in reliability, maintainability, and functional availability

Immunity from high-intensity radiated fields (HIRF)

More hardware and software modularity

Less hardware and software uniqueness

Better growth provisions in the areas of processing throughput and memory capacity

More multifaceted architectural openness for compatibility with growth hardware and software

Improved functional flexibility through onboard software-loading capability

Increased system and functional integration

An example of one of the more advanced avionics programs is the Pave Pace program (see section 3.1.3). In this program, parallel processing is planned for very high processing throughput. In addition, high-speed graphics processing is used to generate real-time panoramic scenes, and advanced radio-frequency signal processing permits better data extraction and correlation. A fault-tolerant architecture is used along with extensive built-in test capability. The result is improved system reliability, functional availability, and maintainability.

9.4. Information Age

Today's avionics systems provide flight crews with large amounts of data. Future systems will continue to generate more and more data. In addition, airborne datalinks and ground-based gatelinks will also add to the information flow to the flight deck. Too much data can lead to information overload for pilots. As new avionics capability is added to aircraft, the resulting information must be managed in ways to avoid increased crew workload and possible data disorientation.

Avionics designers are well aware of the need for intuitive situation display formats of information and are taking steps to manage avionics-generated information better. Another form of information, however, is not uniquely related to avionics. It includes the kinds of information that flight crews traditionally use in the form of manuals and other paper documents. Manuals can be cumbersome to carry and difficult to use, and the other miscellaneous assortment of documents can be difficult to organize and manage. The goal of the avionics information age is to reduce paper documentation in the cockpit and to help users manage, access, and present information more effectively. The decade of the 1990s will see significant progress in this goal.

Electronic library systems (ELSs) are envisioned as mass storage systems and repositories for documents such as flight manuals, nav chart data, maintenance manuals, and even passenger entertainment data. The electronic library first and foremost must provide quick access to information. By reorganizing information into structures that permit quick electronic access, ELS makes needed information more readily available. Designers may develop several different topic-based tree structures for information access. These tree structures could be based on different views of the same information. For example, actual and forecast weather information could be stored in the ELS for multiple users: flight, maintenance, and cabin crews as well as passengers. For the flight crew, the access tree would be based on the operational need for flying efficiently, avoiding severe weather, and complying with FAA and company regulations. For example, correlation of the weather reports with federal regulations and company policies would facilitate the flight crew's understanding of the weather implications to the current flight. For maintenance crews, the same weather information could be organized with an access tree that correlates the weather reports with minimum equipment dispatch requirements for the flight's weather conditions. Similarly, the access tree for the cabin crew could correlate the weather reports with the projected food and entertainment schedules to maximize passenger comfort. Passengers could access actual and forecast weather information for their vacation or business destinations. Suffice it to say that electronic library capability will permit easier and faster access to information, with appropriate electronic links to relevant cross-references. The high-resolution displays associated with ELS will permit more graphic presentations of information.

In the long term, navigational data, such as the air route structure and terminal procedure data (departures, arrivals, approaches), will be stored in data records in the ELS. Then, each element (navaids, intersections, altitudes, headings, frequencies, operating minimums, etc.) will be available to the flight management system (FMS), the electronic display system, and other systems. This will permit the flight crew to select a specific procedure and load it as part of the continuing flight route. The FMS can then generate 3-D flight-director steering commands for the crew to follow, or the FMS can be coupled to the flight control system for automatic execution of the procedure. Alternatively, the crew could choose to fly the procedure manually and have the FMS monitor their nav track and altitude accuracy. The crew would select tolerance limits (e.g., a half mile for track, a hundred feet for altitude) and an alert would be sounded if a tolerance limit is reached. The crew would be able to select appropriate com frequencies (ATIS, approach, tower, etc.) associated with the procedure via menu choices instead of by keying in the frequency.

ELS represents the general trend in avionics today for more information management, correlation, validation, distribution, and availability. This trend is being fueled largely by the trend toward higher levels of system integration.

9.5. Integration

The general trend for modern avionics systems is for higher levels of system and functional integration. One level of hardware integration occurs at the device level, where several circuit-stage elements are integrated to eliminate wire interconnections, to increase miniaturization, and to improve performance and reliability. Examples include VHSIC technology (see section 2.3.2), surface-mount devices (SMDs), multichip modules, and application-specific integrated circuits (ASICs). Data buses provide a different form of integration—the sharing of information between subsystems for mutual benefit. Another form, which avionics designers will explore and emphasize more fully in the 1990s, will be achieved by overlapping or combining common types of functions and combining closely associated functions at the subsystem level.

Figure 9.1 shows some functional associations. Note that at the core of this diagram is a common fail-operational power supply that serves all of the functions. It eliminates the need for a discrete power supply for each separate function and ensures that a power supply failure will not cause functional loss. Some functions perform similar tasks, such as the ACARS/AVPAC datalink, satcom datalink, and the Mode S datalink. These functions have some similar circuitry. Consolidating these circuits saves size, power consumption, and weight.

The onboard maintenance system (OMS) and airplane condition monitoring system (ACMS) also have similarities. They both must have broad connectivity with other avionics units in order to collect data. The OMS continuously collects status information representing the health of other systems. The ACMS also collects system data, typically upon some predetermined condition. For example, engine parameters may be stored by the ACMS as a snapshot of data at the condition of full-thrust power and gear-up. This kind of information is later off-loaded and analyzed to detect functional degradation. Both the OMS and ACMS collect and store large amounts of systems data. The mechanisms for doing this can be consolidated for the resulting savings.

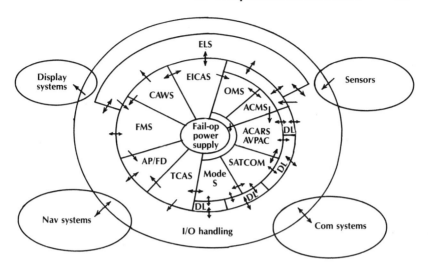

ACARS Aircraft communications, addressing and reporting system
ACMS Airplane condition monitoring system
AP/FD Autopilot/flight director
AVPAC Aviation VHF packet communications
CAWS Caution and warning system
CMU Communications management unit
DL Datalink
EICAS Engine-indicating and crew-alerting system
ELS Electronic library system
FMS Flight management system
I/O Input/output
Mode S Selectively addressable transponder
OMS Onboard maintenance system
TCAS Traffic-alert and collision-avoidance system

Figure 9.1. Subsystem associations

The engine-indicating and crew-alerting system (EICAS) and caution and warning system (CAWS) also monitor system parameters to detect functional failures. However, unlike the OMS, which has as its primary responsibility the isolation of a failure to a single LRU, the EICAS and CAWS detect failed operational capability and annunciate flight deck effects to the crew. The systems' similar tasks suggest some amount of consolidation. Other systems are associated in the following ways:

The flight deck effects annunciated by EICAS and CAWS need to be tagged to LRU failures isolated by the OMS.
The FMS drives the autopilot/flight director with steering commands.

The Mode S transponder is the communications link between TCAS and data provided by other aircrafts' transponders.

In the future, TCAS may drive the autopilot and/or flight-director system directly with collision-escape commands.

Both the ELS and the various datalink systems provide access to information. Maintaining an association between these systems will improve information retrieval for users.

Some level of integration is possible in each of these examples.

Other associations are also suggested in figure 9.1. Each of the peripheral subsystems (nav, com, display, sensors) depicted in this figure can be viewed as a center for subsystem integration. For example, sensors such as radar, infrared, air data, and optical imaging provide information about the aircraft's external environment, so they have some level of functional and hardware commonality. This commonality is where integration can occur to facilitate the fusion of the sensor data. Likewise, nav, com, and display subsystems each have a level of commonality where integration can occur. Avionics designers are reviewing the costs and benefits of higher levels of integration in these and other areas for future systems.

Figure 9.2 shows the relationships between pilot responsibilities and avionics functional categories. The pilot's responsibilities are to aviate (fly the airplane in a stable, safe way), navigate, and communicate and manage the systems, the aircraft, and other aspects of the flight. The four major categories of avionics help pilots meet each of these responsibilities.

Looking along the main diagonal of figure 9.2, one sees the traditional aircraft control instruments, nav systems, com systems, and major managing systems (including integrated display systems). It is the off-diagonal cells of the matrix, though, that are most interesting and relevant to the trends of advanced avionics. As an example, note that fly-by-wire (FBW) capability appears at the intersection of control support systems and the "communicate" responsibility. This suggests that the pilot's responsibility to communicate control intentions to the airplane's aerodynamic surfaces (e.g., ailerons and elevators), traditionally accomplished via cables and hydraulically boosted pushrods, is being displaced by electronic signals through FBW capability. So FBW can be thought of as a new, off-diagonal avionics capability. Another example is automatic dependent surveillance (ADS), placed at the intersection of nav systems and the communicate responsibility. The rationale for this placement is that, at least in areas without ATC radar coverage, the pilot has the responsibility to inform (communicate) ATC of the airplane's location (nav position). With ADS capability, onboard-determined posi-

Pilot Responsibilities / Avionics Categories	Aviate	Navigate	Communicate	Manage
Control support systems	ADI, DG ALT, VSI, IAS	DG, HSI RA, GPWS TCAS, EVS	FBW	AP, AFCS AFDS, TMS
Navigation systems	DG, HSI RA, GPWS TCAS, EVS	VOR, DME, ADF ILS, MLS, GPS INS, LORAN, WxR	ADS TCAS	FMS RNAV
Communication systems	FBW	ADS TCAS	VHF, satcom datalink transponder	ATN
Avionics management systems	AP, AFCS AFDS, TMS	FMS RNAV	ATN	AP, FCS, AFDS FMS, ATN EFIS, EICAS

Figure 9.2. Relationships between avionics categories and pilot responsibilities (a list of acronyms and abbreviations appears at the back of the book).

tion (dependent surveillance) is automatically communicated to ATC. TCAS is another example of a relatively new avionics capability that fits into an off-diagonal cell. It appears in the same cell as ADS because it involves the automatic communication of positions of other nearby aircraft (nav-related information).

The matrix in figure 9.2 is simply a tool for thinking about new avionics capabilities. Other analysts may place new capabilities in different cells; that is not important. The important thing is to stimulate thinking and analysis of these off-diagonal avionics capabilities. Studying pilot needs and responsibilities within the context of avionics categories may uncover new integrated capabilities that will meet a need in a beneficial way. Some of the hallmarks of system integration include better performance, higher accuracy, and more efficient resource sharing. The integrated com, nav, and IFF avionics program ICNIA (see section 3.1.4) is a good example of highly integrated configurable modules that result in good functional availability, fault tolerance, and graceful degradation.

The U.S. Air Force ATF program (see section 3.2) and the U.S. Army RAH helicopter program (section 3.2) both involve high levels of integration of sophisticated subsystems. As such, they serve as good examples of the benefits and pitfalls associated with the cutting edge of integration. Common to both aircraft is the fault-tolerant Pave Pillar architecture (see section 3.1.3). Pave Pillar involves a high level of system integration for information correlation and consolidation. This integrated capability is partitioned into reconfigurable common modules using VHSIC technology (section 2.3.2). The modules are integrated with high-speed fiber-optic data buses. The result again is high availability and graceful degradation of the avionics functions, better system capability, increased reliability and maintainability, and reduced pilot workload.

It is somewhat ironic that integration, while making more information available to flight crews and thereby increasing their workload, at the same time makes automation possible, which reduces crew workload.

9.6. Automation

Automation in aviation dates back to the Wright brothers and their automatic stability augmentation system, but they could never have envisioned the breadth and depth of today's automation. The trend toward higher levels of integration is making possible more and more automation for the often-mentioned benefits of improved functional performance, increased safety, and better-managed crew workload. The higher systems interaction permitted by integration also permits better functional capability and better data correlation. A natural derivative of this is the possibility of increased levels of functional automation.

Since systems have more access to data and can typically monitor and process this data more effectively than the human operator, and since system automation can have better performance capability than the human, automation is a natural consideration. Automated systems do not always have better performance capability; they do not have human judgment, for example. Autofeathering propellers and electrical load shedding are examples of useful automatic capability. Nevertheless, there is a significant downside to relegating some aircraft operational functions to automatic systems. As flight crews depend more on improved and, in some cases, superior-to-human capability of systems, their skill and proficiency levels decrease along with their attentiveness, making the crew less effective when quick and accurate responses are needed the most.

It is very important, therefore, for systems designers to permit close-coupling of the human crew with the information and control loop. There is a tradeoff here in that the more involved the pilots are with information processing and decision making, the higher is their workload. Attempts to reduce workload through automation have sometimes resulted in reducing pilot's situation awareness. It is very important to keep the crew in the functional loop. The role of the automatic systems should be to monitor and cue the crew and intervene automatically only when the crew cannot act fast enough or assimilate enough of the relevant combinations of information to analyze the situation correctly with an adequate response time. Where automation is used, human-system cooperative capability should be built in. There must be a mechanism for the system to inform the crew of its status and for the crew to inform the system of their intentions and wishes. This application of automation is called human-centered automation. Human-centered automation emphasizes system operational aspects such as workload management and optimization, taking into consideration human performance limitations and capabilities.

By the late 1990s more of the air traffic control (ATC) system will be automated in order to handle increased traffic levels safely. The automated systems will communicate directly with onboard computers via datalink. The onboard crew will be in this data-transmission loop to review received messages as well as messages generated by onboard systems to be sent to ATC. There is a risk, though, that if the crew is permitted fewer autonomous actions and they merely monitor and accept automatically generated messages, they may not be closely enough in tune with the flight activity for deep situation awareness. They would be exercising less judgment and would be bound by more decision-making constraints.

Studies have shown that people are not very good at monitoring automatic activity or detecting rare events, such as failures. These are precisely the events that require alertness and quick, accurate reaction on the part of the crew. Automatic systems lack the creative problem-solving skills and judgment of alert, skilled crewmembers. With their speed and precision, however, the systems can outperform humans in monitoring aircraft functions.

Automation will be increased to meet the needs of future increases in traffic densities. That is, as traffic densities increase, airplanes will be operating closer together, and the precision of automation will be required for safety. In some areas, or at some times when ATC services are reduced, pilots may be less able to cope if they become too dependent on automatic systems. System operational flexibility needs to be retained to permit pilots to deal effectively with airborne emergencies or critical flight situations.

Several military programs are analyzing the human-system interface issues in order to optimize both sides of this interface. For example, the army's RAH program (see section 3.2) has as part of its goal optimizing the pilot-in-the-loop concept through MANPRINT (manpower and personnel integration). MANPRINT is a human factors program that focuses on crew-system relationships. The Pilot's Associate program (section 3.1.5) uses an expert systems (ES) approach to automating some functions for workload reduction. The intent is to keep the pilot in the loop by having the systems provide recommendations and situation awareness information. Likewise, the Supercockpit program (section 3.1.6) also involves a human-machine study and ES approach to situation analysis and advice. The Pave Pace program (section 3.1.3) uses artificial intelligence (AI) neural networks with adaptive learning capability to provide decision-making assistance to the pilot.

In the future we will likely see some amount of responsibility shift from pilot decision making to ATC system and controller decision making, and from pilot actions to automatic-system actions. To the extent that this happens, flight crews will need more frequent training in manual procedures and more knowledge of system capability and limitations. Even today's modern, automated, envelope-protected, fly-by-wire aircraft are not failure-proof or human-proof, and pilots must remain alert and on guard against system aberrations or their own operational mistakes.

Avionics designers must find ways of keeping flight crews more involved as the need for automation increases. Avionics designers must become more aware that there is a kind of automation that improves situation awareness and there is a kind that diminishes this awareness. The challenges for avionics designers are many:

- Improving information sorting, correlation, consolidation, and presentation to the flight crew
- Providing human decision-making interfaces with the onboard systems
- Providing situation-managing capability for flight crews
- Providing good crew-intervention mechanisms in automatic functions
- Designing automation to support, rather than displace, the flight crew

These improvements must be accomplished without creating unacceptable workload and information overload.

9.7. Postscript

Avionics trends are inextricably dependent on highly dynamic technological advances, government stimulation and regulation, international air traffic management, airspace system compatibilities, and the general business and economic climate. These diverse factors play an important role in the direction and extent of evolving avionics advances.

Despite the obvious complexities, the engineering of modern avionics systems, both at the concept level and at the implementation level, is improving and progressing rapidly. Designers are emphasizing quality, reliability, maintainability, testability, and usability. They are making significant systems advancements by taking more of a top-down approach to concept, definition, design, and implementation. The design process is being supported by better requirements-analysis tools. The development process is being supported by standardized software-engineering techniques and computer-aided software design, development, and test tools. The entire avionics industry is reaching a better understanding of the pros and cons of system integration and automation. When this understanding is coupled with the design trends in advanced avionics, the result will be avionics capability undreamed of only a few years ago.

Avionics trends are evolving as technological improvements are made. It is interesting to monitor the avionics field while looking for paradigm shifts. A paradigm is a framework establishing the way things are done. Joel Barker indicates in his book *Discovering the Future* (1989, 16) that "while trends are important, they are almost always instigated by a paradigm shift. By understanding the way paradigms change, we can better anticipate the future." The technology shift from analog to digital circuitry was a paradigm shift that resulted in a major change in the way avionics were designed and developed. It resulted, as well, in new functionality and improved performance. Likewise, the advent of the microprocessor resulted in new and more powerful avionics capability and functionality—a paradigm shift. In the future it is possible that large-scale flat-panel displays will result in another paradigm shift. The observer of trends in advanced avionics must watch closely for these paradigm shifts and their effects on avionics functionality.

ACRONYMS and ABBREVIATIONS

AAS Advanced automation system; part of future NAS

ACARS Aircraft communications, addressing, and reporting system

ACAS Airborne collision-avoidance system; term used in Europe instead of TCAS

ACF Area control facility (consolidated terminal and enroute ATC facility)

ACMS Airplane condition monitoring system

ADA DOD-developed high-level language; ANSI-MIL-STD-1815A

ADC Air data computer

ADF Automatic direction finder

ADI Attitude director indicator

ADIRU Air-data and inertial-reference unit

ADOCS Advanced digital optical control system

ADS Automatic dependent surveillance; associated with satcom

AEEC Airlines Electronic Engineering Committee; part of ARINC

AERA Automated enroute ATC program

AFCS Automatic flight control system

AFDS Autopilot flight director system

AFWAL Air Force Wright Aeronautical Laboratories

AGL Above ground level

AI Artificial intelligence

AIMS Airplane information management system; integrated modular cabinet; part of Boeing 777

Aircom Datalink service provided by SITA; compatible with the ACARS datalink provided by ARINC in the United States

ALPA Air Line Pilots Association

ALT Altimeter; altitude

AM-LCD Active-matrix liquid-crystal display

AMSC American Mobile Satellite Corporation

ANSI American National Standards Institute

AOC Airline operational communications

AOPA Aircraft Owners and Pilots Association
AP Autopilot
APC Aeronautical passenger communications
ARINC Aeronautical Radio, Inc.
ARTCC Air route traffic control center; U.S. enroute ATC facility
ARTI Advanced rotorcraft technology integration; associated with the RAH-66 helicopter program
AS Airspeed
ASD Aeronautical Systems Division (U.S. Air Force) at Wright-Patterson Air Force Base
ASE Aircraft survivability equipment
ASI Airspeed indicator
ASIC Application-specific integrated circuit
ATA Air Transport Association; advanced tactical aircraft (U.S. Navy)
ATARS Automatic traffic-advisory and resolution service
ATB Advanced technology bomber
ATC Air traffic control
ATCRBS ATC radar beacon system
ATF Advanced tactical fighter; next-generation fighter (U.S. Air Force)
ATIS Automatic terminal information service
ATM Air traffic management
ATN Aeronautical telecommunication network
ATS Air traffic service
AVPAC Aviation VHF packet communications; binary-oriented form of the ACARS character-oriented protocol
AVRADA Avionics Research and Development Activity; U.S. Army, Ft. Monmouth, N.J.
AvSat Aviation Satellite Corporation
AX Next-generation fighter (U.S. Navy)
BAe British Aerospace
BCAS Beacon collision-avoidance system
BIT Built-in test
BPS Bits per second
CAD Computer-aided design
CAM Computer-aided manufacturing
CASE Computer-aided software engineering
CAWS Caution and warning system
CDU Control display unit; primarily associated with FMS
CFPD Command flight-path display
CISC Complex instruction set computer
cm Centimeter
CMU Communications management unit

CNI Communication, navigation, and identification; also called CNP and CNS

CNP Communication, navigation, and pulse

CNS Communication, navigation, and surveillance

CPU Central processing unit

CRT Cathode ray tube

CSP Common signal processor

DABS Discrete-address beacon system

DARPA Defense Advanced Research Projects Agency

dem/val Demonstration and evaluation

DFCS Digital flight control system

DG Directional gyro

DH Decision height

DIP Dual inline package

DL Datalink

DME Distance-measuring equipment

DME-P Precision DME

DOD Department of Defense

DOT Department of Transportation

EADI Electronic ADI

EAP Experimental aircraft program; associated with EFA program

ECAM Electronic crew-alerting and monitoring; also called electronic centralized aircraft monitor; similar to EICAS

ECL Emitter-coupled logic

EFA European fighter aircraft

EFIS Electronic flight instrument system; includes PFD, ND, and usually MFD

EHSI Electronic HSI

EICAS Engine-indicating and crew-alerting system

EL Electroluminescent

ELS Electronic library system

EMI Electromagnetic interference

EMP Electromagnetic pulse radiation

ES Expert systems

ESA European Space Agency

ESM Electronic support measures; also called electronic surveillance measures

ETA Estimated time of arrival

ETOPS Extended-range twin-engine operations

EVS Enhanced vision system

EW Electronic warfare

FAA Federal Aviation Administration

FADEC Full-authority digital engine control
FANS Future Air Navigation Systems; an ICAO committee
FBL Fly-by-light; fiber optics
FBW Fly-by-wire
FCC Federal Communications Commission; flight control computer
FCS Flight control system
FDDI Fiber Distributed Data Interface; a fiber-optic bus
FDS Flight director system
FE Flight engineer
FLIR Forward-looking infrared
FMGCS Flight management guidance and control system
FMS Flight management system
FPV Flight path vector
FSD Full-scale development
FSS Flight service station
FSX Fighter support experimental; joint program between the United States and Japan
GaAs Gallium arsenide
GAMA General Aviation Manufacturers Association
G force Gravitational pressure caused by accelerations resulting from airplane maneuvering
GLONASS Global orbiting navigation satellite system; Russian satnav
GNSS Global navigation satellite system
GPS Global positioning system
GPWS Ground-proximity warning system
GRANAS Global radio navigation system
GS Groundspeed; glideslope (part of ILS)
HDSM High-density standard modules (ICNIA common modules)
HERF High-energy radiated-electromagnetic field (HIRF is preferred)
HF High frequency
HIRF High-intensity radiated fields
HMD Helmet-mounted display
hr Hour
HSCT High-speed civil-transport program
HSI Horizontal situation indicator
HUD Head-up display
IAP Instrument approach procedure; commonly called an "approach plate"
IAS Indicated airspeed
IC Integrated circuit
ICAO International Civil Aviation Organization
ICNIA Integrated communication, navigation, and identification avionics

IEEE Institute of Electrical and Electronics Engineers
IFF Identification friend or foe; military ATC transponder
IFR Instrument flight rules
ILS Instrument landing system
IMA Integrated modular avionics
IMC Instrument meteorological conditions
INEWS Integrated electronic warfare system
Inmarsat International Maritime Satellite Organization
INS Inertial navigation system
I/O Input/output
IOC Initial operational capability
IRAD Independent research and development
IRS Inertial reference system
IRST Infrared search and track (radar)
IRU Inertial reference unit
ISO International Standards Organization
JIAWG Joint Integrated Avionics Working Group (tri-service)
JTIDS Joint tactical information-distribution system
kHz KiloHertz
kts Knots
LCD Liquid crystal display
LED Light-emitting diode
LHX Light helicopter experimental; later changed to RAH (U.S. Army)
LLTV Low-light television
LLWAS Low-level windshear-alerting system
LNAV Lateral-steering navigation mode; controls aircraft heading
LOC Localizer (part of ILS)
LORAN Long-range navigation; low-frequency navigation system
LPI Low probability of intercept (radar)
LRM Line-replaceable module; language reference manual
LRU Line-replaceable unit
LSI Large-scale integration
MANPRINT Manpower and personnel integration; military human factors program
MB Marker beacon (part of ILS)
Mbps Megabits per second
MCP Mode control panel
MEP Mission equipment package; associated with U.S. Army RAH-66 program
MFD Multifunction display
MHz MegaHertz
MIMIC Microwave/millimeter-wave monolithic integrated circuit; same as MMIC

min Minutes

MIPS Million instructions per second

MLS Microwave landing system

MMIC Microwave and millimeter-wave integrated circuits; same as MIMIC

Mode S Aircraft transponder that ATC can selectively address

MOPS Minimum operational performance standards; RTCA document

MSL Mean sea level

MTBF Mean time between failure

MTBUR Mean time between unscheduled removal

NAS National airspace system

NASA National Aeronautics and Space Administration

NASP National airspace system plan; National Aero-Space Plane

NATF Navy advanced tactical fighter

Navsat Proposed European satellite nav system

Navstar Navigation by timing and ranging

NBAA National Business Aircraft Association

NOE Nap-of-the-earth; low-altitude flight capability

ND Navigation display (part of EFIS)

NDB Nondirectional beacon

NOTAM Notice to airmen

nm Nautical miles

NVPS Night-vision pilotage system; associated with U.S. Army RAH-66 program; also called PNVS

OMS Onboard maintenance system; ARINC Project Paper 624

OSI Open systems interconnection

OTH Over-the-horizon (radar)

PFD Primary flight display (part of EFIS)

PI Parallel interface bus; used in highly integrated modular systems

PLA Programmable logic array

PNVS Pilot night-vision system; also called NVPS

PPS Precise positioning service; related to GPS

RA Radio (or radar) altimeter

RAH Reconnaissance attack helicopter (U.S. Army)

R & D Research and development

RF Radio frequency

RFDF Radio-frequency direction finder

RISC Reduced instruction set computer

RLG Ring-laser gyro

RMI Radio magnetic indicator

RNAV "Random" or area navigation

RNPC Required navigation performance capability; a FANS committee specification

RPV Remote-piloted vehicle
RTCA Radio Technical Commission for Aeronautics
RTP Radio tuning panel
RVR Runway visual range
SAE Society of Automotive Engineers
SAI Systems Architecture and Interfaces; a subcommittee of AEEC
satcom Satellite communication
satnav Satellite navigation
SDI Strategic Defense Initiative
sec Seconds
SID Standard instrument departure; an IFR procedure
SINCGARS Single-channel ground and airborne radio system
SITA Société Internationale de Telecommunications Aeronautiques
SMD Surface-mount device
SMT Surface-mount technology
SPS Standard positioning service; related to GPS
SSR Secondary surveillance radar
STAR Standard terminal arrival route; an IFR procedure
STARS Stored terrain and access retrieval system
TACAN Tactical air navigation
TCA Terminal control area; a type of controlled airspace around high-density airports
TCAS Traffic-alert and collision-avoidance system
TDMA Time-division multiple-access
TDWR Terminal Doppler weather radar program
TFEL Thin-film electroluminescent
TF/TA Terrain following, terrain avoidance (radar)
TIMATION U.S. Navy satellite navigation system
TM Test/maintenance bus
TMS Thrust management system
TNAV Time-steering navigation mode; uses aircraft speed adjustments to achieve predetermined waypoint arrival times
TRANSIT U.S. Navy satellite navigation system
UHF Ultrahigh frequency
USAF U.S. Air Force
VFR Visual flight rules
VHF Very high frequency
VHSIC Very high speed integrated circuit
VISTA Very intelligent surveillance and target acquisition
VLSI Very large scale integration
VLF Very low frequency
VMC Visual meteorological conditions

VNAV Vertical-steering navigation mode; controls aircraft climb and descent
VOR VHF omnirange
VSI Vertical speed indicator
WxR Weather radar
XPNDR Transponder

REFERENCES

Air Force Magazine. 1991. *Aerospace World,* June, 13–14.

Barker, Joel Arthur. 1989. *Discovering the Future.* St. Paul, Minn.: ILI Press.

Baud, Pierre. 1988. Fly-by-Wire Controls: The New Airliner Standard. *ICAO Bulletin,* Mar., 19–22.

Birch, Stuart. 1989. International Viewpoints—Automation. *Aerospace Engineering,* Feb., 39–40.

Borky, Lt. Col. John M. 1987. Integrated Avionics: Watershed in Systems Development. *IEEE AES Magazine,* Nov., 10–15.

Brahney, James H. 1988. High Tech Help for the Combat Pilot. *Aerospace Engineering,* Aug., 15–18.

Canan, James W. 1984. Toward the Totally Integrated Airplane. *Air Force Magazine,* Jan., 34–41.

———. 1989. Technology Hits the Cost Barrier. *Air Force Magazine,* May, 38–42.

Castellano, Robert N. 1986. VHSIC Program Spurs U.S. IC Technology. *Defense Electronics,* July, 114–27.

Colucci, Frank. 1986. LHX Decisions. *Defence Helicopter World,* Feb.–Mar., 36–41.

Condom, Pierre. 1987. Airborne Navigation Plots Its Future. *Interavia,* Aug., 850–56.

Dornheim, Michael A. 1986. Crew Situational Awareness Drives Avionics Developments. *Aviation Week & Space Technology,* June 23, 114–16.

———. 1992. FAA Flight Tests to Measure Synthetic Vision Performance. *Aviation Week and Space Technology,* Jan. 20, 41.

Dudney, Robert S. 1989. The ATF and Its Friends. *Air Force Magazine,* Jan., 46–53.

Dugan, Thomas D. 1989. Gallium Arsenide Up to Speed. *Electronic Engineering Times,* Mar. 27, 60.

Eydaleine, Genevieve. 1988. Navigation by Satellite—the Next Step for Civil Aviation. *ICAO Bulletin,* Mar., 16–18.

FAA. 1987. *National Airspace System Plan,* Apr.

———. 1989. *National Airspace System Plan,* Sept.

———. 1990. *Aviation System Capital Investment Plan,* Dec.

Federal Radionavigation Plan. 1988. *Avionics,* May, 30–32.

Federal Radionavigation Plan—Part 2. 1988. *Avionics,* June, 10–17.

Federal Regulatory Directory. 5th ed. 1986. Washington, D.C.: Congressional Quarterly Inc.

Fellman, Lynne, and Ernest Lucier. 1989. Transponders: The Mode S Datalink. *Avionics,* Oct., 14–18.

Geisenheyner, Stefan. 1989. Current and Future Developments in Cockpit Design. *Armada International,* Mar., 52–64.

Gelsinger, Patrick P., Paolo A. Gargini, and Gerhard H. Parker. 1989. Microprocessor circa 2000. *IEEE Spectrum,* Oct., 43–47.

George, Fred. 1988. Challenger 601-3A. *Business & Commercial Aviation,* Oct., 102–7.

Giordano, John. 1988. Silicon-on-Silicon Makes Today's Technology Seem Primitive by Comparison. *Rockwell News,* Dec., 1–4.

Global Plan for Communications and Navigation. 1988. *Avionics,* Oct., 8–12.

Green, David. 1988. At the (Sidearm) Controls of Boeing's Light Hawk. *Rotor & Wing International,* Jan., 38–132.

Harris, Robert L. 1988. Integrated CNI Avionics: The Customer's Perspective. *IEEE AES Magazine,* July, 2–9.

Henderson, Breck W. 1991. Exotic Materials to Boost Speed of Next Generation of Computers. *Aviation Week & Space Technology,* Apr. 15, 66–67.

Hofmeister, Ernst. 1989. Microelectronics 2000. *Telcom Report,* Dec., 43–46.

Holt, Daniel J. 1985. General Aviation Avionics: An Overview. *Aerospace Engineering,* Apr., 10–23.

Hopkins, Harry. 1988. MLS – Pie in the Sky? *Flight International,* Mar. 19, 22–24.

Hughes, David. 1989. Glass Cockpit Study Reveals Human Factors Problems. *Aviation Week & Space Technology,* Aug. 7, 32–34.

Hutchinson, J. E. 1989. The Hybrid Landing System – An Airline Pilot's View. *SAE Technical Paper,* #892377, Sept. 25–28, 1–4.

Joss, John. 1987. Cockpit Automation. *Defense Electronics,* May, 63–79.

Kmetz, Allan R. 1987. Flat-Panel Displays. *IEEE AES Magazine,* Aug., 19–24.

Labich, Kenneth. 1987. Boeing Battles to Stay on Top. *Fortune,* Sept. 28, 64–72.

Lacagnina, Mark M. 1986. TCAS on Trial. *AOPA Pilot,* Dec., 61–62.

Lauber, John K. 1989. New Philosophy Needed for Cockpit Automation. *Avionics,* Feb., 8–9.

Leary, William M., ed. 1989. *Aviation's Golden Age.* Iowa City: University of Iowa Press.

Lenorovitz, Jeffrey M. 1988. Authorities Address Europe's Air Traffic Control Crisis. *Aviation Week & Space Technology,* June 6, 86–87.

Lerner, Eric J. 1986. Toward the Omnipotent Pilot. *Aerospace America,* Oct., 18–22.

Lowenstein, George, John Phanos, and Edward Rish. 1988. Sole Means Navigation in U.S. Navy Aircraft. *IEEE AES Magazine,* Aug., 16–22.

Marsh, George. 1987. Navigation in the '90s. *Defence Helicopter World,* Oct.–Nov., 21–26.

McLaren, Grant. 1988. CAE Advances State-of-Art in Computer-Generated Images. *Professional Pilot,* Dec., 92–94.

Messina, Andrew. 1989. Technology Management for the 1990s. *Manufacturing Engineering,* June, 49–51.

Moxon, Julian. 1989. U.S. Technology on the Critical List. *Flight International,* June 17, 59–62.

Murphy, E. A. 1987. Wind-Shear Recovery: Keep the Thrust Up and the Nose Up! *ICAO Bulletin,* Apr., 11.

Naegele, Tobias. 1989. Ten Years and $1 Billion Later, What Did We Get From VHSIC? *Electronics,* June, 97–103.

NASA. 1988. Some Basic Issues in Cockpit Automation: A Human Factors View. *Callback,* Feb.

Nelms, Douglas W. 1988. Fly by Light. *Professional Pilot,* Jan., 20–23.

Nordwall, Bruce D. 1988. GPS Applications, Production Grows as System Gains Acceptance. *Aviation Week & Space Technology,* Oct. 31, 83–85.

_____. 1989. Navy Chooses LCD Technology for New A-12 Color Displays. *Aviation Week & Space Technology,* Sept. 4, 56–57.

_____. 1991. Flight Tests Highlight New GPS Uses, Emphasize Need for GPS/ GLONASS System. *Aviation Week & Space Technology,* Dec. 2, 71–73.

Perry, Tekla S., and Paul Wallich. 1985. Computer Displays: New Choices, New Tradeoffs. *IEEE Spectrum,* July, 52–66.

Pohlmann, Lawrence D., and J. Roland Payne. 1988. Pilot's Associate Demonstration One. *IEEE AES Magazine,* Aug., 3–9.

Poradish, Frank. 1987. Modular ICNIA Packaging Technology. *IEEE AES Magazine,* June, 20–23.

_____. 1988. Trends in Modular Avionics Packaging. *Avionics,* May, 8–10.

Rawles, James W. 1988. High Wire Acts. *Defense Computing,* Jan.–Feb., 42–45.

_____. 1989. VHSIC Forges Ahead. *Defense Electronics,* Jan., 61–74.

Rhea, John. 1986. The Most Integrated Avionics System Ever. *Interavia Aerospace Review,* Oct., 1211–13.

_____. 1988. Fly by Light. *Air Force Magazine,* Mar., 98–103.

Rickey, Patricia. 1987. Foul-Weather Friend: Color Airborne Radar. *Rotor & Wing International,* Apr., 38–40.

Ross, Douglas T., John B. Goodenough, and C. A. Irvine. 1975. Software Engineering: Process, Principles, and Goals. *Computer,* May, 17–27.

Rowe, Jeffrey. 1990. New Building Blocks for Future Architectures. *Defense Electronics,* Nov., 31–34.

Schroen, Walter. 1988. Chip Packages Enter the 21st Century. *Machine Design,* Feb. 11, 137–43.

Scott, William B. 1989. Simulator, Flight Tests Validate Integrated Pictorial Cockpit Display. *Aviation Week & Space Technology,* Jan. 9, 51–53.

Shearer III, Oliver V. 1986. Technology in the Cockpit. *Journal of Electronic Defense,* Oct., 99–104.

Sutton, Oliver. 1989. Swissair is First with All–Category 3 Fleet. *Interavia Aerospace Review,* Apr., 315–17.

Sweetman, Bill. 1989. B-2 Bomber for the 21st Century. *Interavia Aerospace Review,* Jan., 22–26.

_____. 1991. YF-22 Faces Budget Battle. *Interavia Aerospace Review,* June, 57–61.

Sweetman, Bill, and Mark Hewish. 1988. Airborne Navigation. *International Defense Review,* Jan., 35–39.

Thompson, Ken. 1988. Notes on "The Electric Control of Large Aeroplanes." *IEEE AES Magazine,* Dec., 19–24.

Timmerman, Kenneth R. 1987. The EFA Takes Off. *Defense Electronics,* Sept., 95–128.

Tippins, Mac. 1988a. TCAS Too. *Professional Pilot,* Oct., 12.

_____. 1988b. The Progress of TCAS 2. *Professional Pilot,* Oct., 62–64.

Voelcker, John. 1988. The Iffy Orient Express. *IEEE Spectrum,* Aug., 31–33.

Warwick, Graham. 1988. Military Avionics: The Right Stuff? *Flight International,* Oct. 15, 22–24.

Washington Information Directory 1987–1988. 1988. Washington, D.C.: Congressional Quarterly Inc.

Williams, Tom. 1989. Flat-Panel Displays Come on Strong in Speed, Resolution and Color. *Computer Design,* Feb. 1, 65–82.

INDEX

ACARS. *See* Aircraft communications, addressing, and reporting system
Ada programming language, 30, 32, 61, 68, 77
ADS. *See* Automatic dependent surveillance
Advanced tactical aircraft (ATA), 62, 82
Advanced tactical fighter (ATF), 47, 51, 53, 60–62, 82, 85, 94, 147, 148, 154, 169
Advanced technology bomber (ATB), 62–63
AERA. *See* Automated enroute air traffic control system
Aeronautical Radio, Inc. (ARINC), 39, 50, 131, 136–37
Aeronautical telecommunication network (ATN), 138–39, 158, 159
Aircraft communications, addressing, and reporting system (ACARS), 23, 131, 138, 143, 158, 166
Airmass navigation, 18, 124–25
Air traffic control
    automation, 14, 171
    environment, 14–19, 48, 88, 130, 133, 140, 161
ARINC. *See* Aeronautical Radio, Inc.
Artificial intelligence (AI), 27, 33–35, 49, 50, 53, 57, 59, 74, 82, 87, 101, 109, 111, 127, 161, 172
ATA, 62, 82
ATB, 62–63
ATF. *See* Advanced tactical fighter
ATN. *See* Aeronautical telecommunication network
Autoland, 69, 149–51, 154, 158, 159
Automated enroute air traffic control system (AERA), 14–19, 41, 48, 49, 88, 89, 120, 132

Automatic dependent surveillance (ADS), 135–37, 143, 157, 159, 163, 168
Automation, 13, 84–90, 104, 109, 170
    functional, 13, 84, 106, 109, 162, 170
    human-centered, 88, 111, 160, 163, 171
    monitoring, 13–14, 48, 90
    preemptive, 14
AVPAC datalink, 131, 138, 139, 158, 166
AX. *See* Advanced tactical aircraft

Boeing 777 aircraft, 67–70, 81
Buses
    architecture, 21, 166
    ARINC-429, 21–22
    ARINC-629, 22, 49, 68, 69, 77
    FDDI, 23
    high-speed, 23, 49, 52, 60, 65, 67, 73, 83, 170
    MIL-STD-1553, 21–22, 77
    MIL-STD-1773, 22, 49
    optical, 22, 49, 52, 53, 60, 62, 65, 67, 160, 162, 170

Collision-alerting, 11, 97, 115, 125, 128, 129, 133, 139–43, 154
Control-display unit (CDU), 92–100, 106, 110, 160

Datalink, 10, 69, 130–31, 143, 158, 159, 162, 164, 168, 171
Digital map, 43, 73, 100, 111, 124, 148, 160

EFA, 66–67
EFIS. *See* Electronic flight instrument system

EICAS. *See* Engine-indicating and crew-alerting system
Electronic flight instrument system (EFIS), 19–20, 94, 121, 127
Electronic library system (ELS), 23, 69, 108, 132, 165, 168
Engine-indicating and crew-alerting system (EICAS), 14, 85, 96, 108, 167
Enhanced vision system, 123–24, 158, 159
European fighter aircraft (EFA), 66–67
Expert systems (ES), 33–35, 50, 56, 74, 82, 109, 111, 161, 171, 172

FANS. *See* Future air navigation systems (FANS) committee
FBW. *See* Fly-by-wire
Federal Aviation Administration (FAA), 36, 38, 140, 142
Fighter Support Experimental (FSX), 48, 72
Flat-panel displays and technology, 20–21, 46, 49, 61, 62, 65, 68, 69, 74, 94, 160, 162, 173
Flight control system (FCS), 71, 77, 154, 158, 165
Flight management system (FMS), 13, 68, 69, 77, 78, 165, 167
Fly-by-light (FBL), 61, 71, 147–48, 154, 158, 159
Fly-by-wire (FBW), 11, 61, 62, 63, 65, 66, 68, 69, 72, 74, 144–47, 153, 154, 158, 159, 162, 168
FMS. *See* Flight management system
FSX, 48, 72
Future air navigation systems (FANS) committee, 42, 118, 136–37, 163

Gallium arsenide devices, 25–26, 29, 49, 61, 72, 126
Global navigation satellite system (GNSS), 117, 159, 163
Global positioning system (GPS), 10, 42, 65, 67, 68, 69, 112, 113, 114–18, 122–23, 127, 163
approach guidance, 122–24
differential, 122–23, 124, 128
GLONASS, 116, 118, 163
GNSS, 117, 159, 163
GPS. *See* Global positioning system

Head-up display (HUD), 61, 66, 88, 97, 105, 107, 123, 158
Helmet-mounted display (HMD), 57, 58, 61, 64, 65, 66, 97, 111
High-speed civil transport (HSCT), 70–72
HUD. *See* Head-up display

ICAO, 39–40, 50, 112, 117, 120, 122, 136–37, 139, 163
ICNIA, 24, 53, 54–55, 61, 65, 66, 73, 81, 82, 169
ILS, 41, 120–22
IMA. *See* Integrated modular avionics
Inertial system, 113, 116, 118, 119
INEWS. *See* Integrated electronic warfare system
Inmarsat, 42, 46, 136
Instrument landing system, 41, 120–22
Integrated electronic warfare system (INEWS), 61, 65, 66, 82
Integrated modular avionics (IMA), 24, 47, 52, 67, 68, 69, 73, 79–81, 160, 162
Integration
functional, 47, 68, 75, 127, 164, 166
hardware, 75, 76, 166
software, 76
system, 43, 47, 52, 54, 64, 71, 75–84, 89, 125, 154, 162, 163, 164, 166, 169

Joint integrated avionics working group (JIAWG), 60, 65

Lateral navigation (LNAV), 13
LCD. *See* Flat-panel displays and technology
LHX. *See* Reconnaissance attack helicopter
LNAV, 13
LORAN-C, 39, 46, 112, 114, 116, 127

MANPRINT, 63, 110, 171
Microwave landing system (MLS), 10, 16, 41–42, 67, 68, 78, 114, 120–22, 124, 128, 157, 162
Millimeter-wave radar, 123
MIMIC, 28, 61, 62, 126
MLS. *See* Microwave landing system
Mode S. *See* Transponder
Multichip modules, 29

NASP, 70–72, 148
NATF, 62, 82. *See also* Advanced tactical fighter
National Aero-Space Plane (NASP), 70–72, 148
National airspace system plan, 14, 112

Onboard maintenance system (OMS), 23, 68, 69, 166
Open systems interconnection (OSI), 23–24, 47, 131, 134, 137, 139, 159, 160
Operational simplicity, 12, 104–110, 111, 160, 161
OSI. *See* Open systems interconnection

Pave Pace, 53–54, 73, 164, 172
Pave Pillar, 23, 24, 51–52, 60, 64, 65, 73, 82, 169
Pave Sprinter, 53, 73
Pentagon critical technologies plan, 37
Pilot's Associate, 56–57, 58, 61, 74, 104, 109, 171

Reconnaissance attack helicopter (RAH), 58, 63–66, 82, 94, 110, 147, 169, 171
Reduced instruction set computer (RISC) technology, 25–26, 49, 60
RTCA, 39, 50, 134, 139, 140

SAE, 39
Satcom, 42, 46, 69, 129, 134–38, 139, 143, 157, 158, 159, 162, 166
Satnav, 113, 114–18, 157, 162
Sidestick controller, 65, 147, 148–49, 153
Situation awareness, 54, 56, 61, 68, 74, 78, 88, 89, 94, 97, 99, 107, 110, 133, 156, 160, 161, 163, 170, 171, 172
Situation displays, 107
SMT, 29, 55, 166
Software engineering, 31–32, 49, 173
computer-aided (CASE), 33, 50
Speech recognition and synthesis, 35, 49, 50, 58, 61, 65, 66, 67, 74, 91, 101, 103, 111, 160
Supercockpit, 57–59, 61, 64, 74, 94, 99, 103, 109, 172
Surface-mount technology (SMT), 29, 55, 166
Synthetic vision system, 71, 123, 158

TCAS, 17, 40–41, 77, 129, 133, 140–42, 143, 153, 158, 162, 168, 169
Touchscreen, 102
Transponder, 127, 129, 139, 142
Mode S, 41, 132, 140–42, 168
Mode S datalink, 15, 17, 41, 88, 89, 129, 132–34, 138, 139, 143, 158, 166
Trends
automation, 13, 14, 85, 87, 88, 89
business, 47
device-level, 26–29, 43
evolutionary, 82, 162–64, 173
general avionics, 48, 60, 78, 81, 84, 89, 91, 92, 94, 95, 96, 112, 126, 127, 129, 153, 154, 156–61, 166, 168, 172, 173
integration, 21, 24, 76, 77, 79, 170

Vertical navigation (VNAV), 13
VHSIC technology, 27–28, 43, 49, 52, 53, 55, 60, 61, 62, 65, 66, 73, 126, 166, 169
Virtual imaging and control, 58, 103, 104, 111, 160
VNAV, 13
Voice recognition. *See* Speech recognition and synthesis

Weather radar, 126
Windshear detection, 11, 41, 101, 149, 151–53, 154, 155, 157, 158, 159
Workload management, 6, 8, 10, 12, 14, 20, 34, 56, 57, 61, 64, 68, 77, 84, 86, 90, 92, 94, 97, 101, 103, 104–11, 132, 143, 149, 157, 160, 161, 164, 170, 171, 172

X-30. *See* National Aero-Space Plane